ILLUSTRATIONS FROM
BIBLICAL ARCHAEOLOGY

D. J. WISEMAN

THE TYNDALE PRESS · 39 BEDFORD SQUARE · LONDON W.C.1

TO MY WIFE

WITHOUT WHOSE ENCOURAGEMENT
THIS BOOK WOULD NEVER HAVE BEEN WRITTEN

Made and printed in England by
STAPLES PRINTERS LIMITED
at their Rochester, Kent, establishment

CONTENTS

PREFACE 5

I. THE DAWN OF CIVILIZATION . . . 7

II. THE PATRIARCHAL AGE 23

III. EGYPT AND THE EXODUS 33

IV. IN THE DAYS OF THE KINGS 51

V. THE EXILE AND AFTER 69

VI. IN NEW TESTAMENT TIMES 79

VII. METHODS AND RESULTS 95

BIBLIOGRAPHY 103

GENERAL INDEX 110

I. *Figure of a high-ranking Egyptian nobleman wearing a tight-fitting, pleated linen garment with wide skirt.*

c. 1400 BC. Wood. 12½ in. high. BM 2320.

3

ACKNOWLEDGMENTS

Permission to reproduce illustrations is gratefully acknowledged to the following:

American Schools of Oriental Research (fig. 74); Ashmolean Museum, Oxford (5, 7); Vorderasiatisches Museum, Berlin (67-69, 102); The Trustees of the British Museum (all BM figs.); British School of Archaeology in Iraq (43, 61, 108); Brooklyn Museum (31); Cairo Museum (40); Fogg Museum of Art, Harvard (82); Hebrew University, Jerusalem (75, 112); Iraq Museum (13-14); Istanbul Museum (52, 56, 101); Dr. Merrill N. Isely (79); Musée du Louvre (24, 26, 48, 78); Metropolitan Museum of Art, New York (27, 72); Oriental Institute, Chicago (47, 73); Palestine Archaeological Museum (55, 65); Trustees of the Wellcome-Marston Research Expedition (64, 65, 111).

I am particularly indebted to Mr. B. Butler who has been responsible for all the art-work, to Mr. R. Inchley who first envisaged the book in this form, to Miss M. Morss for typing the manuscript, and to my wife for much help in many ways.

PREFACE

Archaeology is at present a popular subject for study and widespread attention is paid to its discoveries. The mass of evidence from countries named in the Bible is growing so rapidly, however, that it is often difficult for the student and teacher of biblical history, literature and theology to keep abreast of the new knowledge. At the same time development in the methods used in the archaeological sciences makes it necessary to reconsider some earlier conclusions. Thus, as in any progressive science, there is always place for a new presentation of archaeological results for the general reader.

'Biblical archaeology' has now become a specialist branch of archaeological research requiring competence in both archaeological and biblical studies. It selects from the material remains of ancient Palestine and its neighbouring countries any evidence which may bear upon the biblical narrative. More than twenty-five thousand sites, only a few score of which have been excavated, and almost a million written documents, many unpublished, are the primary sources from which the manners and customs, language and history, peoples and places of the ancient Near East are being revealed. On the basis of this evidence it is now possible to paint a picture of Old Testament times on a canvas which a hundred years ago was almost a blank. Much has an indirect bearing and here the

2. *Relief portrait of the Assyrian king, Sargon II, conqueror of Samaria in 723/2 BC.* Khorsabad. 723/2–705 BC. Gypsum. 8 ft. high. BM 118822.

5

archaeologist relies on a comparison of general ideas, historical phases or customs. Direct, factual coincidence between the extra-biblical and biblical sources is, however, much more rare, and is mainly to be found in contemporary documents which name a person or place known from the Bible itself. It is within this latter sphere that confirmation of the biblical narrative is to be expected and is found.

This book seeks to present those items which directly relate to both Testaments, together with a selection of those which generally illustrate some aspects of the biblical era. Emphasis has been placed on photographs of the objects, some published here for the first time. These, as well as illustrating the actual text, may prove helpful to teachers. For the same reason special attention has been paid to the scripts employed during the biblical period. Photographs must always be, however, a poor substitute for the objects themselves, many of which can be seen in the British Museum, or in similar collections elsewhere. Any Bible student will find that time taken to study objects from the ancient Near East will be well spent.

Limitations of size prevented any attempt to make this book an exhaustive treatment of the subject. The specialist student is well served by many books written to illustrate the bearing of archaeology on the history, text, and to a lesser extent the religious ideas of the Bible. A number of these are listed in the detailed Bibliography which has been included in order to encourage the student to explore further in this modern field of research and discovery which conditions so much of our present understanding of the Bible's history and times.

3. *Black obelisk showing Jehu of Israel bowing before Shalmaneser III, king of Assyria. See also figs. 50-51.*
Nimrud. 841 BC. Limestone. 6 ft. 6 in. high.   BM 118885.

6

CHAPTER I

THE DAWN OF CIVILIZATION

Archaeological researches show that the first traces of civilized man are to be found in the ancient Near East. Prehistoric remains at Jericho (Jordan), Byblos (Lebanon), Jarmo, Hassuna and Ubaid (Iraq) show that village sites flourished before 4500 BC, though little is yet known of this period compared with the surprisingly fully developed life of the city-states which flourished in ancient Sumer, north of the Persian Gulf, in the following millennium.

Among the traditions of the Sumerian peoples are several which allude to the introduction of civilization, the creation of man and of animals, and to the beginnings of the arts and crafts. The most complete version of the Creation Epic has survived on a series of seven, originally six, clay tablets commonly named after the opening words *Enuma elish*, 'when on high' (fig. 4). In these they state their view of the origin of the universe and of man, the whole creation being a divine act *ex nihilo*. The first tablet describes the time when the heavens and earth did not exist, when there were no plants or food, when the watery deep or 'chaos' was the source and origin of everything. The newly created gods representing order and system were, however, soon opposed by rebellious elements whose plottings were overheard by the god Ea and defeated. In revenge

4. *The third tablet in the Assyrian series relating the story of Creation. This copy, made for the Assyrian Royal Library at Nineveh, bears a text similar to the older Babylonian versions which in part may be traced to Sumerian originals in the third millennium BC.*

Nineveh. *c.* 650 BC. 3½ in. × 2¼ in.
BM 93017.

7

the rebels, led by Tiamat, created monstrous forces under a god Kingu. Eventually another god, Marduk, the champion of good and justice, defeated Tiamat in a stiff battle. He split her in half like an oyster, forming the heavenly firmament with the upper and the earth with the lower half (fourth tablet). The fifth tablet outlines the creation of the stars to mark the passing of time, and of the moon to regulate the reckoning of the days, implying that the luminaries preceded the creation of plant and animal life. Man, according to the sixth tablet, was the final and special creation by the god Marduk, formed from the blood of the slain Kingu mixed with earth's clay or dust, and made for the service and worship of the gods. The seventh tablet is a hymn added later to exalt Marduk as the head of the Babylonian pantheon in the second millennium.

The differences between this epic and the Hebrew accounts of creation (Genesis i, ii) are too numerous for the Genesis story to have evolved from the Babylonian. Any similarities with the Genesis record have to be rescued from the overlaying extraneous matter which forms the bulk of the poem; such can best be explained as due to both versions going back to common primary facts. The biblical record with its lofty conception of God bears a dignity unparalleled in any other account.

Among early Sumerian texts are a number of 'genealogical tablets' written in the staccato style of which Genesis i-xi is reminiscent. Some provide an extra-biblical parallel to Genesis v, listing the ten 'great men' who ruled before the flood, naming in the list those who from other texts are claimed to be historical persons. One prism inscription (fig. 5) gives these early ancestors ages which make the biblical figures seem almost insignificant, the individual ages varying between 21,600 and 10,800 years. The lists agree with the Bible that it was the tenth who

5. *Sumerian prism naming the ten kings who ruled before the flood.*
Kish. *c.* 2000 BC. 8 in. × 3¼ in.   Ashmolean Museum, Oxford (WB 444).

survived the great flood. WB 444 reads 'then the Flood swept over the earth. After the Flood had swept over kingship was sent down (again) from heaven'. This clear break in history is marked in these inscriptions by a line drawn to divide the text from that describing post-diluvian events.

Recently published Sumerian texts provide earlier parallels to the Hebrew account of paradise and of the fall than was hitherto possible. One describes the original 'organization of the earth and its cultural processes' whereby Enki, the god of wisdom, established law and order, setting bounds for the sea and winds, and giving directions for building, husbandry and productivity in general. The same myth is preserved in the Berossus account of Oannes, the god who daily taught the newly created inhabitants of Babylonia the knowledge of writing, numbers and arts of every kind, including agriculture, husbandry (the naming of animals) and architecture, necessary to civilized life for men living in the plain (Sum. *edinna*; Heb. *eden*). Another Sumerian text describes the paradise at Dilmun (Persian Gulf), which was naturally irrigated by fresh water (so Genesis ii. 6). Here birth was without pain or travail until Enki was smitten with a deadly curse after eating eight plants. Another text, also a copy dating from the early second millennium, describes the special creation of Woman who is named *Nin.ti*, a Sumerian expression which can be equally translated 'the lady of the rib' and 'the lady who makes live' which recalls Eve, 'the mother of all living', fashioned from Adam's rib.

Allusions to man's rebellion against the gods, resulting in the flood, may indicate that the Sumerians knew of some event whereby man fell from his original state. Certain elements in the account of Genesis iii occur in the earliest written texts and stone engravings. Symbols including the sacred tree and serpent are found in prehistoric seals. The cylinder-seal (fig. 6) of the Third Dynasty of Ur (*c.* 2000 BC) which has been said to

6. *Impression made by a cylinder-seal engraved with a scene representing two figures seated by the side of a sacred tree, or date palm; behind the figure on the left is a serpent. It has been suggested that this scene refers to a Babylonian version of the Temptation of Eve (Genesis ii. 4-iii. 24), but no cuneiform text in support of this view is known.*

c. 2000 BC. Green Schist. $1\frac{1}{16}$ in. high. BM 893260.

represent the 'Fall' or 'Temptation of Eve' is, however, probably only a pure coincidence of symbolism. The two beings, both males and deities, who are portrayed seated on either side of a fruit-bearing tree with a serpent erect behind one of them, can be given a very different explanation from other religious texts and scenes in which they recur.

More than half a million clay documents inscribed in the cuneiform (wedge-shaped) script have been recovered from the ancient Near East and almost half of these date from before 1800 BC. The earliest of these so far known is a small polished limestone tablet found at Kish, near Babylon, in 1922 and dated c. 3300 BC (fig. 7). The inscription cannot be read although the individual pictographic signs are clear (e.g. head, foot, hand and numerals). The direction in which the signs are to be read or which side of the tablet the inscription commences is not certain. The difficulty of reproducing curved lines on clay soon led to the simulation of the pictograph in a linear script using a square-ended stylus made of wood, bone or reed (fig. 8). As with the earliest tablet, the inscription, dated c. 3100 BC, appears to be an account or record of property and to include a personal name. These clay tablets precede the earliest writings on papyrus from Egypt which are dated c. 2800 BC. A table showing the development of the cuneiform script is given on page 24.

Writing is also very relevant to our subject for the following reason. Other forms of archaeological evidence are important for any understanding of the history and life of biblical times and places, but often the remains of buildings, art, and the varied artifacts which result from most excavations, will depend upon contemporary writings to turn them from merely general to specific and direct illustrations of the Bible, itself a written record. Moreover, Palestine, for reasons of geography, topography and climate, as well as perhaps archaeological accident, has as yet yielded few ancient documents. From the pre-Christian era these are, with few and unusual exceptions like the Dead Sea Scrolls, inscriptions

7. (*Left.*) *The earliest Sumerian inscription employing a pictographic script. The contents are as yet unread.*

From Kish (nr. Babylon). *c.* 3300 BC. Limestone. 2¾ in. × 2¾ in. Ashmolean Museum, Oxford. BM (Cast) No. 116630.

8. (*Right.*) *Clay tablet inscribed in linear characters immediately derived from pictographs. Account of fields, crops and commodities.*

Jemdet Nasr (nr. Kish). Pre-dynastic (*c.* 3100 BC). 3⅛ in. × 2⅞ in.   BM 116730.

9. *Plan of the world showing the surrounding oceans and marking Babylon on the River Euphrates as the centre. The distant mountainous districts beyond the seas, as well as Assyria and the swamps at the mouth of the River Euphrates, are shown.*

The map was drawn to illustrate the campaigns of Sargon of Agade c. 2300 BC. This king penetrated Asia Minor and his exploits, recorded in the preceding text, were already well known throughout western Asia by the fifteenth century BC. It is an example of early geographical knowledge (cf. Genesis x).

Sippar. 6th century BC. 3¼ in. × 4⅝ in.

BM 92687.

on stone, clay tablets and potsherds. The more fragile papyri have seldom survived. For this reason most of the documentary biblical parallels come from neighbouring countries. The fact that writing is found there at an early date makes it likely that the scribal art was not unknown in Palestine about the same time.

In December 1872 George Smith, an Assistant at the British Museum, published a *Chaldaean Account of the Deluge* based on his work on the Museum's large collection of inscribed clay tablets brought from the royal library of Ashurbanipal at Nineveh, mostly dated from the seventh century BC. He had discovered a series of texts giving the adventures of Gilgamesh, an early post-diluvian king of Erech, in which the eleventh tablet was devoted to an account of the flood (fig. 10). Smith produced good evidence to show that the epic had been copied or adapted from a legend composed at 'a very early period'. His view was subsequently proved correct by the discovery of an Old Babylonian version of the same epic dated *c.* 1700 BC and then in 1914 by the publication of an older Sumerian prototype in the University Museum in Philadelphia. It is now known that the flood story was an independent piece of literature prior to 2000 BC and was only later incorporated into the Gilgamesh Epic cycle. At the same early date there were already references to the flood in other texts (cf. fig. 5).

The eleventh tablet tells how Gilgamesh, in quest of eternal life, is told a story by one Uta-napishtim. The gods determined to send a deluge which would cover the earth and obliterate all mankind, but the god Ea revealed their plan to Uta-napishtim, a native of Shuruppak, who, following divine instructions, built a ship to enable him, his family and animals to escape the flood waters which came upon them from above and below. Under the guidance of a pilot, Puzur-Amurru, the giant barge survived the storm, winds, rain and floods which covered the tops of the mountains. After drifting for some time the vessel grounded on Mt. Nisir

10. *The eleventh tablet of the Assyrian version of the Epic of Gilgamesh which records the Babylonian account of the flood. Versions of this Epic date from the late third millennium BC. A fragment found recently at Megiddo shows that the Epic was known in Palestine in the fourteenth century BC.*

Nineveh. *c.*650 BC. 5⅜ in. × 5⅞ in. BM K3375.

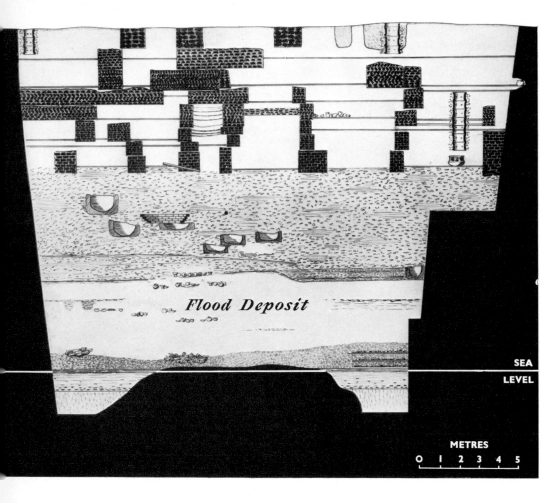

Flood Deposit

SEA
LEVEL

METRES
0 1 2 3 4 5

11. *Traces of an unusual, but probably local, flood were found at Ur by Sir Leonard Woolley in 1927. The flood deposit is clearly marked by the absence of debris in the water-deposited clay. Note, in contrast, the numerous objects and graves discovered and marked in the earlier (upper) levels.*

12. *(Right.) Statue of a he-goat standing on its hind-legs with fore-legs in a branch of a tree. Probably a holder for an incense or offering-bowl. This remarkable piece, typical of the finest craftsmanship of the third millennium BC, is made of gold (legs and face), silver (belly), lapis (horns, eyes and upper fleece), and white shell (lower fleece) on a wooden core. This object is sometimes erroneously called 'The Ram caught in a thicket'.*
Ur. c. 2500 BC. 18¼ in. high.   BM 122200.

(cf. 'one of the mountains of Urartu', Genesis viii. 4) and Uta-napishtim released a dove to test the abating waters. As the dove returned a swallow was despatched later. When a raven finally flew off and, finding a resting place, did not return, Uta-napishtim left the ship with his family and the beasts to sacrifice to the gods who, despite some misgivings, confer immortality upon him. The resemblances of this story to Genesis vi–ix are obvious, though the major part of the poem is far different, and it is still not known how the biblical and Babylonian accounts may be related historically.

The excavations by the British Museum and the University Museum of Philadelphia led by Mr. (later Sir) C. L. Woolley at Ur near the Persian Gulf in 1922–34 led to an interesting discovery in 1929. While making a number of soundings down to virgin soil a clean riverine deposit of clay measuring eight to eleven feet deep was encountered (fig. 11). The deposit was not, however, found in all the pits made and the excavator considers it to have been laid by an unusually great flood where the waters have left silt on the slope of a hill in part of the town. Woolley himself equates these traces of a heavy local deluge with that mentioned in the Gilgamesh Epic and in the historical texts, and dates them after the first pottery-bearing levels (Al 'Ubaid) and before the first written records. Similar bands of clay deposits were found by Langdon at Kish, sixty-five miles to the north, in the same year, but these appear to be of an earlier date. Marks of local inundations have been found at other sites which do not coincide with those at Ur and many problems, particularly of the extent and chronology, remain unsolved. Recent opinion places the flood tradition back in the late Stone Age when its more widespread character could have resulted in the diffusion of the flood story among many races.

The excavations at Ur are, however, best known from the discovery of the Royal Graves which furnish examples of the art and culture which flourished there at the end of the Early Dynastic period (c. 2500 BC), that

13. *The helmet found in the grave of Mes-kalam-shar. It was worked from a single sheet of 15-carat gold and originally worn attached by laces through the eyelets on the rim to an inner woollen cap, traces of which were found. A similar helmet can be seen on the mosaic standard (figs. 16, 17).*
Ur. *c.* 2500 BC. 9 in. high.   Iraq Museum.

14. *Gold dagger and sheath found with a belt in a grave at Ur. The gold blade is inscribed with the mark of a craftsman or the owner. The hilt is of lapis-lazuli studded with gold and the sheath of gold filigree work imitates an earlier reed pattern.*
Ur. *c.* 2500 BC. 14½ in. long. Iraq Museum.

is half a century or more before Abraham. The finest of the later graves, dug down into the shafts cut to house the royal tombs, belonged to Mes-kalam-shar and was found in the season 1927-8. The coffin lay surrounded by upright spears and in it the position of the body of this noble could be traced only by the magnificent gold helmet (fig. 13) which still covered the rotting skull. At the waist a golden dagger had hung. Inscribed bowls, lamps and other objects in precious metals attest the wealth of the time and a standard of workmanship rarely surpassed in later ages.

Within the sixteen brick-vaulted tombs in the main cemetery were found human victims, varying in number from six to eighty in a single tomb group, sacrificed to accompany and serve the owner in the next life. From one of these graves comes the famous Ur dagger (fig. 14) with its blade of gold and hilt of lapis-lazuli studded with gold, and sheath in open work designed to imitate a natural weave. Queen Shubad had been buried in her fine jewellery (fig. 15), accompanied by numerous female attendants in similar garb. A choir of ten had been accompanied on a golden harp (now in the Iraq Museum), and the bodies of groups of servants, of soldiers and of two asses show that the royal corpse had been ceremonially transported into the tomb on a wooden sledge before both attendants and treasures had been sealed in. King Abargi had been buried with similar honours. Many of the royal tombs had been plundered in antiquity, but in the dark corner of one there remained the 'mosaic standard' (figs. 16, 17) which was lifted by the excavators intact and now remains a silent witness to a civilization only hinted at in Genesis v.

The *ziggurat*, or temple-tower, was a dominant feature of the ancient city of Ur. The original construction by Ur-Nammu, *c.* 2100 BC, consisted of baked clay bricks banded with bitumen mortar, forming three

15. *The intricate head-dress and ornaments of gold leaf, lapis-lazuli and carnelian, of Queen Shubad of Ur (shown on reconstructed model head).*

Ur. *c.* 2500 BC.   University Museum, Philadelphia.

17

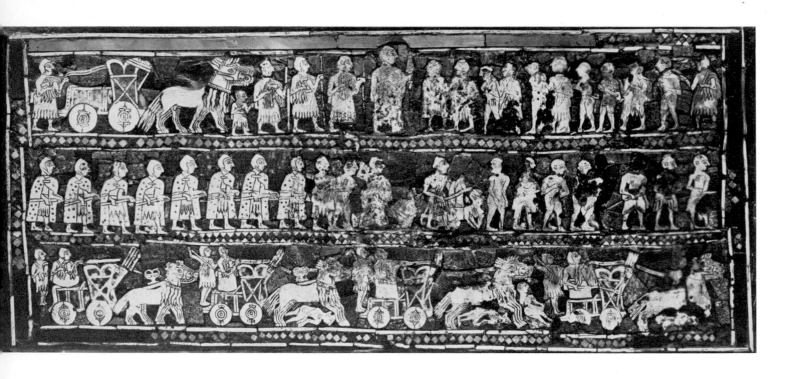

16, 17. *Both sides of a pictorial mosaic standard of lapis-lazuli and shell set in bitumen on wood. On the left the upper register shows the Prince (large figure), the royal family, chariot and prisoners. The middle register depicts soldiers and prisoners, and the lower,*

Sumerian chariotry. On the right a prince feasts with courtiers and receives booty from the enemy. This is a masterpiece of early Sumerian art.

Ur. *c.* 2500 BC. 1 ft. 7 in. long ×8½ in. high.   BM 121201.

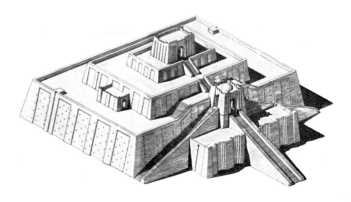

terraces, each of a diminishing size and of a different colour, the uppermost of blue, and surmounted by a small temple of gold and silver. Access was by stairways, and the upper terraces were decorated with trees and plants watered by a special hoist, traces of which can be seen (fig. 18). The 'hanging gardens' at Babylon may refer to similar ornamentation of the temple-tower there. The two remaining lower stages at Ur are 70 ft. high and measure 200 ft. × 150 ft. at the base. When later reconstructed by Nabonidus (550 BC) the ziggurat at Ur was built with seven stages, as had been those at Babylon and Borsippa by Nebuchadrezzar II (605-561 BC). There is no textual support for the view that these ziggurats had any astronomical significance. The tower at Babylon was named *E.temen.an.ki*, 'Building of the Foundation of Heaven and Earth', and its associated temple *E.sag.ila*, 'The temple whose top is heaven'; that at Borsippa was called *E.ur.imin.an.ki*, 'The Building of seven stages of Heaven and Earth'.

The biblical story of the Tower of Babel (Genesis xi) must reflect a time before the sack of Babylon by the Hittites (*c.* 1650 BC), and the existence of a ziggurat there as early as the third millennium BC is very probable. The identification of the vitrified remains of the tower at Borsippa (Birs Nimrud, 7 m. S.W. of Babylon) with the 'Tower of Babel' of Genesis remains questionable. Since cities in Northern Mesopotamia also possessed ziggurats, their existence and even their history could have been known to the Israelites at an early date. It is also suggested that the 'stairway' of Jacob's dream (Genesis xxviii. 12) and the steps up to the altar (Ezekiel xliii. 13-17) are reminiscences of the approach up a ziggurat.

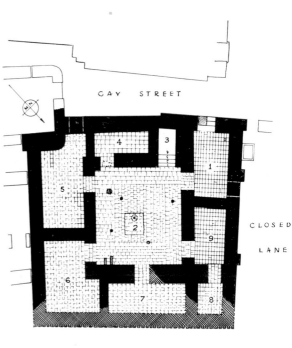

20. (*Above.*) *A house of the Patriarchal period as excavated by Sir Leonard Woolley. The same general layout of private dwellings was in use throughout biblical times. The ground plan (right) shows the single entrance leading from the narrow street into a paved courtyard surrounded on three sides by rooms. There is a place to wash the feet outside the long reception room, the walls of which were whitewashed, a lavatory (4), kitchen (5) and a private chapel and storage space. The brick staircase leads to the upper floor which was supported by arches, traces of which were found in the fallen brickwork.*

No. 3. Gay St., Ur. *c.* 1900 BC.   Excavated 1927.

CHAPTER II

THE PATRIARCHAL AGE

The traditions of the days of the Hebrew patriarchs preserved in the book of Genesis are now considered by the majority of scholars, of various shades of religious opinion, to reflect with remarkable accuracy the actual conditions of the Middle Bronze Age (*c.* 2100–1550 BC) now known independently from archaeological research. At the beginning of this period Ur 'of the Chaldees', from which Terah emigrated with Abraham, was a prosperous city. The high standard of living is reflected both in the fine private houses of the period (figs. 20, 21) and in the numerous inscriptions recovered from the ruins of Ur and recently published. About 1900 BC, when Ur was destroyed, the Semitic Amorites (meaning 'Westerners') rose to power throughout the Middle East. Texts from the archives at Mari (Syria) show that they displaced native governors, and many of the new personal names which now appear are reminiscent of biblical Hebrews, though they cannot be identified with them. The names of Abram, Laban, Zebulun and Benjamin occur, and towns and villages in the neighbourhood of Harran ('Cross-roads'), which flourished at this time, bear names which reflect the families which once occupied them, Turakhi (Terah), Sarugi (Serug), Nahur (Nahor). This accords with the Hebrew tradition which located the ancestral home

21. *Artist's reconstruction of the house at Ur shown in fig. 20. The balcony overlooking the open courtyard gives access to the private rooms and to the flat roof.*

ORIGINAL PICTOGRAPH c. 3500 BC	SIMPLIFIED CHARACTER c. 3000 BC	ARCHAIC SUMERIAN c. 2800 BC	OLD BABYLONIAN c. 1800 BC	ASSYRIAN c. 800 BC	NEO-BABYLONIAN c. 600 BC	IDEOGRAPHIC AND SYLLABIC TRANSLITERATION	MEANING
						KU_6 ḫa	fish
						GUD	ox
						ANŠU	donkey
						ŠE še	grain
						DINGIR an, ìl	god heaven
						UTU ud etc	sun day light
						APIN pin	to till plough
						É bit	house
						LÚ	man

in the Upper Euphrates region (Genesis xxiv. 10) and thought of Abram and his sons as nomadic Aramaeans (Deuteronomy xxvi. 5).

Opinions differ as to the exact date for the Patriarchs. Albright and De Vaux place Abram between 1900 and 1700 BC; Rowley in the eighteenth-seventeenth centuries, and Cyrus Gordon as late as the Amarna Age (fourteenth century). The uncertainty is due in part to the present inability to give a precise date for Hammurabi, the principal Amorite ruler of Babylon. Sidney Smith sets him at 1792-1750 and Albright as 1728-1686 BC. Comparison of the biblical evidence with the mass of contemporary extra-biblical inscriptions furnishes little help except in a general way. The late Middle Bronze IIb period (c. 1750-1550 BC) would seem to fit best with the evidence at present available.

More than one hundred thousand inscribed clay tablets dated to this period have been found. The cuneiform script was used for writing many languages and dialects throughout the ancient Near East all through the second millennium BC when it was also the medium of international communication (fig. 22). Archives from Mari (Tell Hariri) and Alalah (Tell Atshana) in Syria, written in a Semitic dialect virtually identical with that spoken by the Hebrew patriarchs, and from the cities of Babylonia and E. Assyria furnish evidence for the eighteenth and seventeenth centuries. The two succeeding centuries are known from documents from Alalah (later levels), Chagar Bazar and Brak (Syria), Taanach and Shechem (Palestine) and Nuzi (near Kirkuk, E. Tigris). The latter show that the population of the whole area, always a mixture of races, was by this time predominately Hurrian (Horite). Gordon and Speiser have ably demonstrated many parallels between these texts and Genesis xii-xxvi.

It was customary among the Semites and Hurrians of this period for childless folk to adopt a son not only to serve them during their lifetime, but also to provide for their burial and its attendant rites after death. So Abraham chose Eliezer as his first heir, but the adoptee yielded his rights

THE DEVELOPMENT OF
THE CUNEIFORM SCRIPT

22. *The table opposite shows the cuneiform script as used from c. 3500 BC to 75 AD. The non-semitic Sumerians first developed it from curved pictographs (col. i; cf. fig. 7) to a linear form (cols. ii-iii; cf. fig. 8) easier to inscribe on clay tablets with a wood or reed stylus. In the time of the Babylonians and Assyrians (cols. iv-v; cf. fig. 10) the script, in which 600 signs represent both ideas and syllables, was used throughout the Near East for many languages including Hittite (Nasian and Hattic), Hurrian (Horite), Luvian and Urartian. By Nebuchadrezzar's reign the script was much simplified (col. vi; cf. fig. 63). Ugaritic, a Canaanite dialect (see fig. 26), and Old Persian (see fig. 71) employed a modified cuneiform script. The cuneiform script was first deciphered in 1847 (cf. fig. 109).*

to the real heir on the birth of a son (Genesis xv. 2-4). When Sarah gave Hagar to Abraham to provide him with children she was but conforming to the practice of the time. One Nuzi contract states that 'if Gilimninu (the bride) does not bear children, she shall take a Lullu woman (a slave) as a wife for Shennima (the bridegroom) . . . Gilimninu shall not send the handmaid's offspring away.' Abraham may have felt that in driving Hagar out he was breaking the law, until God gave him a special assurance to do so (Genesis xxi. 12). It was a common Hurrian practice for a man to become a servant on the condition that his master provided him with a wife as agreed by contract. So Jacob worked for his brides among the Aramaean tribe of Laban. The important place in law of an oral blessing or death-bed will, as those given by Isaac and Jacob, is confirmed by a case where this was upheld in a Nuzi lawcourt.

The scribes of these 'Old Babylonian' times continued the earlier tradition of preserving, copying and adding to the existing standard works which had been handed down to them by the temple or family. These ancient books included epics and religious and 'scientific' works including lexicography, botany, medicine and law. The well-known 'Code of Laws' promulgated by Hammurabi at Babylon, *c.* 1750 BC, is an example (figs. 23, 24). He took the century-old laws of his predecessors, Lipit-Ishtar of Isin (part of which was found in 1947), Bilalama of Eshnunna and the earlier Urakagina of Lagash, and promulgated a series of case-laws in which the penalties were adapted to the prevailing economic situation. Since provisions in all these groups of laws cover the same field as later Old Testament legislation it is not surprising that significant comparisons may be made. For example, the law of the goring ox in each of these codes is in wording almost identical with Exodus xxi. 28 ff. M. R. Leh-

24. *Hammurabi receiving from the god Marduk the symbols of authority. This scene is sculptured on the top of a stele inscribed with 282 laws.* Susa. *c.* 1750 BC. Diorite. 7 ft. 6 in. high.
Louvre, Paris.

23. (*Left.*) *A portrait of Hammurabi, king of Babylon* (*c.* 1792-1750 BC). *c.* 1760 BC. Limestone. 15 in. wide.
BM 22454.

mann, on the basis of the Hittite code of laws, has shown that a post-1200 BC dating for the narrative of Abraham's purchase of the cave of Machpelah from a Hittite family (Genesis xxiii) must be firmly rejected.

At this time also Egypt controlled the main routes through Palestine to Syria and the freedom of movement and flow of trade is shown by tomb paintings such as fig. 25. Execration texts list the Palestinian towns occupied by Egypt's Asiatic enemies and name, among others, Tyre and Hazor. Excavation shows that Egypt traded with Gezer and Megiddo, two of the Canaanite strongholds at this time. In the south Hebron was unoccupied (so Genesis xxiii. 2), other ethnic groups occupied Jerusalem

25. *A painting from the tomb of Knum-hotep, administrator of the eastern desert. Ibsha, a foreign ruler, arrives in Egypt with thirty-seven 'Asiatics' (Semites) whose multi-coloured garments contrast with the plain white Egyptian*

and Ashkelon, but the area between cities was sparsely populated and enabled the incursion of groups of semi-nomadic Habiru (or 'Apiru; Hebrew and even Arab are probably related terms) among whom must have been the Hebrew Abraham. In the Middle Bronze IIa period (c. 1900-1750 BC) Bethel, Shechem and Dothan and other cities associated with the patriarchs flourished. At Jericho tombs show that desert nomads at this time reoccupied cities that had been allowed to fall into ruins, but the main area of occupation was the hilly central districts of Palestine and the Southern desert (Negeb) which Glueck's survey has proved to have been once thickly populated. Similar surveys show that Moab and

dress. The scene recalls the visit to Egypt of Abraham and Sarah, or of Jacob's sons (cf. Genesis xliii. 11).

Beni-Hasan. c. 1890 BC. 19¾ in. long.

After Lepsius, Denkmäler. II. 133.

Ammon were also inhabited c. 2000 BC, but at the time of the destruction of Sodom, Gomorrah and Zoar, which Kyle and Albright have shown to lie beneath the waters of the Dead Sea, the population hurriedly abandoned adjacent sites and returned to their semi-nomadic life. Sedentary occupation of the country east of Jordan is not found again until the thirteenth century.

The cuneiform texts from Mari, Ugarit, Alalah and Boghazkoi indicate that the larger city-states and tribes were linked by treaties, or 'covenants', defining their boundaries and mutual responsibilities (cf. Genesis xiii, xiv. 13 ff.). One coalition of ten city-states under Hammurabi of Babylon is mentioned. Armies and messengers moved freely and there is nothing improbable in the coalition of kings as given in Genesis xiv, a chapter dated by Albright to the sixteenth century BC. Although the opponents of Abraham cannot be identified with certainty, the personal names (Tudhalia, Ariukku) and place-names fit well into the contemporary picture. The allies followed the 'King's Highway' east of Jordan (Numbers xx. 17), which is marked by a line of forts, the remains of which can be dated to the time before the destruction of Sodom and Gomorrah. The identification of Amraphel with Hammurabi of Babylon is no longer likely. Even if it were possible philologically, other contemporary kings with the same name of Hammurabi ruled at Qatna and Aleppo in Syria.

Religious epics dating from the end of the patriarchal period and written in a local alphabetic script have been found at Ras Shamra, ancient Ugarit. These are of importance for the study of the Canaanite religion and language (fig. 26). In the light of all the archaeological evidence Albright concludes that 'as a whole the picture in Genesis is historical, and there is no reason to doubt the general accuracy of the biographical details and sketches of personality which make the Patriarchs come alive with a vividness unknown to a single extra-biblical character in the whole vast literature of the ancient Near East'.

CHAPTER III

EGYPT AND THE EXODUS

Daily life in ancient Egypt can be profusely illustrated from tomb paintings (fig. 27), papyri and other objects. For some centuries there are, however, few historical texts and Joseph himself lived in one such period known as the Hyksos Age (Dynasty XV-XVI, *c.* 1720-1570 BC). For his life, so vividly described in Genesis xxxix-l, comparisons have to be drawn from earlier or later times when similar customs prevailed.

Soon after 2000 BC Egypt's influence on Syria and Palestine had weakened in face of the pressure from nomadic settlers, themselves driven on by the movements of Hurrians and other groups moving south-west from the Caucasus. By 1700 BC Asiatic foreigners (Hyksos), including large Canaanite and other Semitic elements from Palestine, had overwhelmed the weak rulers of Dynasties XIII-XIV and settled in the Delta of lower Egypt. Their domination may have been partly due to the

27. (*Left.*) *Painting of Egyptian scribes recording the harvest.*
Thebes (Menna Tomb No. 69). *c.* 1420 BC. 1 ft. 3 in. high.

BM (by N. de G. Davies).

28. (*Right.*) *Tomb model of woman carrying basket of food as provision for the dead.*
c. 2000 BC. Painted wood. 1 ft. 3 in. high.   BM 30716.

29. (*Right.*) *Fresco from the tomb of Sebek-hetep (No. 63). The scene, in two registers, shows Semitic envoys from Retenu (Syria) bringing gifts of Phoenician workmanship, gold, silver and bronze vessels, a quiver and a small child. The last envoy (upper register) brings an object which may be either an ivory tusk capped with a small model head of a goddess in gold, or an ointment horn. The white garments, edged in blue and red, are wound below the waist. Other 'Asiatics' are depicted on tomb paintings (see, e.g., fig. 25) or are shown as prisoners on the engravings which celebrate royal victories in the East carved at Thebes, Karnak, Memphis, Beni Hassan, El Amarna and other sites.*
Thebes. Thutmosis IV (1421–1413 BC).
4 ft. 5 in. wide.   BM 37991.

possession of horses and chariots, instruments which Egypt was later to adopt for the reconquest of Palestine. The Hyksos capital was founded at Avaris (Tanis?) about 1720 BC and monuments of this Dynasty are known from the east Delta and upper Egypt. Otherwise little is known of them, for their memory was obliterated by succeeding generations. The paucity of inscriptions may be due to the few excavations so far undertaken on the E. Nile Delta area. Among those which have been found, biblical names like Hur and Jacob occur.

The connection between the Hyksos and the Hebrew settlement in Egypt is now considered almost certain, for numerous details in the Genesis narrative fit in well with comparative Egyptian textual and archaeological evidence. The titles given to Joseph ('overseer over the house', Genesis xxxix. 4, and 'he who is over the house', Genesis xli. 40) may be translations of Egyptian terms in current use. Other inscriptions confirm the titles 'chief of butlers' and 'chief of bakers', and the models commonly placed in tombs, with the intention of enabling the owner to participate in the after-life in the activities represented, include some which illustrate details of the narrative (fig. 28; cf. Genesis xl. 16). The inscriptions show the importance of the magician and the interpreter of royal dreams, and record amnesties for prisoners which were sometimes granted on the king's birthday.

The rise of a Semite to high position in the Hyksos period both was possible and is not without parallel then and in later Egyptian history, when slaves rose to great power in the New Empire (c. 1570–1050 BC), and the advent of Semites at the Egyptian court was no unusual occurrence (fig. 29; cf. fig. 25). In times of famine, some of which are said to have lasted seven years, frontier officials, according to documents dated c. 1350 and 1230 BC, were instructed to allow bedouin from South Palestine to graze their flocks in the Wadi Tumilat (Goshen) area. Joseph's new dignity is clearly defined (Genesis xli. 39–45): as Grand Vizier or Prime Minister

he was ruler, second only to the pharaoh ('king'). His installation into office, at which he received the royal signet ring, fine linen robes and a golden chain, was in accordance with custom. A Theban painting shows Huy, viceroy of Ethiopia, receiving such a ring and an Amarna relief portrays the investiture of Mery-Reʿ by Amenophis IV with a golden chain because 'he had filled the storehouses with spelt and barley'.

Joseph used his new powers wisely. As Prime Minister and 'Superintendent of the Granaries', a high office, he imposed a tax of 20 per cent, the normal for the period, to be paid in grain delivered to the royal granaries situated in each provincial capital. Wooden models of large granaries have been found (e.g. BM 21804). Detailed records of the grain supplies were kept (see fig. 27) and ceremonially reported to the king each year, for the prosperity of the kingdom largely depended on the harvest. One official of this time (cf. fig. 1), Ptah-mose, bore the title 'royal scribe and overseer of the grain supply of the Lord of the two lands'. Another, Baba, tells how 'when a famine arose lasting many years I issued corn to the city in each year of famine'. The breaking up of estates by the use of Joseph's administrative powers accords with the Hyksos period.

The Egyptian inscriptions are, however, mainly of a religious and funerary interest. The oldest corpus, the Pyramid Texts, dating from before 2200 BC, relates the after-life of the pharaoh and the Coffin Texts from the Middle Kingdom (2050-1750 BC) do the same for nobles. Another important sacred book, of which many variants exist, is the collection of magical spells known as the Book of the Dead. The Ani papyrus is the most perfect and longest text of this type from the Theban period (fig. 30). Such rolls of inscribed papyri were commonly buried

30. (*Left.*) *Judgment scene from the Papyrus of Ani, a royal scribe and governor of the granaries. The heart is weighed in the presence of Osiris.*
Thebes. *c.* 1300 BC. 15 in. high. (Total length 76 ft.)   BM 10470.

32. *The Rosetta Stone. The same text is inscribed in hieroglyphs (upper), in a cursive form of hieroglyphs (centre) and in Greek (lower). Through the recurrence in six places of a similar group of signs written within an oval cartouche Thomas Young deduced several letters and read the name of Ptolemy. By 1822 a Frenchman, Champollion, read another name as Cleopatra and formulated a correct system of Egyptian decipherment.*

The dated inscription lists the royal titles and epithets of Ptolemy V (Epiphanes), king of Egypt, and enumerates the benefits the king had conferred on the land. It also lists eight decrees, passed by the priests on the anniversary of the king's coronation, aimed at 'increasing the ceremonial observances of honour which are paid to Ptolemy, the ever-living, in the temples'.

Rashid, Egypt (1798). 195 BC. Black basalt. 3 ft. 9 in. high.   BM 24.

with the dead since they include prayers and hymns whereby the dead could overcome in the underworld and arrive at the 'fields of peace'.

Egyptian literature includes prophecies and wisdom literature with which comparisons with Hebrew literary forms are made. But a most striking example comes from a recently published papyrus now in the Brooklyn Museum and illustrates Joseph's early life (fig. 31). The broken text bears on one side a prison register of about a hundred years before Joseph's time (assuming this to be *c.* 1700 BC), and shows the prison system of the day. The verso lists seventy-nine servants in an Egyptian household, forty-five of whom are 'Asiatics', probably sold into Egypt as slaves, as was Joseph about forty years after the list was written. Some of them bear good Hebrew names like Shiphrah and Menahem. In addition to the names, their office (e.g. 'chief over the house', 'house servant') is listed in the second column and the sex of the slave is noted (third column).

There are descriptive stories among the Egyptian papyri, one the tale of Anubis and Bitis, two brothers, one of whom resisted a woman's seduction and was then forced to flee when she complained of maltreatment, an episode similar in a number of details to the biblical tale of Joseph and Potiphar. About this time also long and descriptive narratives are found in cuneiform literature of which the history of Idrimi of Alalah and the tale of the poor man of Nippur, found near Harran, are later examples. Many Egyptian texts have been published since the discovery in 1799 of the Rosetta stone (fig. 32) led to the decipherment, in 1822, of the hieroglyphic script, used like printed characters for all formal inscriptions. This was mainly the work of Young and Champollion following their identification of the royal names of Ptolemy and Cleopatra written within an oval or cartouche, by comparison with the Greek text.

The religious life of Egypt in the second millennium was dominated by the priesthood of the god Amun, and Joseph's marriage with a priest's

33. *When the Israelites at Sinai turned to the worship of a golden calf it may have represented the god Apis, the bull(-calf) of Memphis.* 4th century BC. Bronze. 6 in. long.

BM 37448.

34. (*Left.*) *Colossal head from the statue of Amenophis (Amen-hetep III), king of Egypt c. 1413–1377* BC, *once thought to be the pharaoh (king) at the time of the Israelite Exodus. He wears the uræus, symbol of sovereignty.*
W. Thebes. XVIIIth Dynasty. Sandstone. 3 ft. 10 in. high.   BM 6.

35. (*Right.*) *One of a number of statues of Rameses II, possibly the pharaoh of the Exodus. Bearded, and wearing a heavy wig on which rests the double crown of Upper and Lower Egypt, he holds the flail in his right hand and the sceptre in his left. His name and title is inscribed on the shoulder:*

Elephantine. 1301–1234 BC. Granite. 5 ft. high.   BM 67.

daughter from Heliopolis (On) was no doubt in keeping with the requirements of his position. Considerable emphasis was placed on the worship of animals (fig. 33) or of deities thought to indwell them, and the ethics and morality of the day were vitiated by magic.

The Hyksos rule was terminated by Amosis I, founder of Dynasty XVIII, who captured Avaris and defeated the retreating Hyksos forces at Sharuhen in Palestine about 1570 BC. The capital was moved back to Thebes and under the energetic Tuthmosis III (*c.* 1500–1450 BC) the Egyptian empire stretched from Nubia to the Euphrates river. Semites moved freely into Egypt and Egyptians are found in many of the larger cities of Syria and Palestine, but with concentration, as would be expected, in such military outposts as Bethshan.

His son Amenophis III enjoyed a peaceful reign after initial campaigning (fig. 34). This king was formerly thought by some to be the pharaoh of the Exodus, but this view is increasingly discredited by more recent archaeological discoveries. The contact between Egypt and Asia resulted in a continuation of the process of religious syncretism begun with the Hyksos. Ba'al, Horon, Resheph and the goddesses Astart, Anath and Asherah were worshipped sometimes under Egyptian names. About 1370 BC the young Amenophis IV (the self-styled Akhenaten) broke the power of the priests of Amun at Thebes by substituting the monotheistic solar worship of Aten and by the removal of his capital to Amarna. But it is impossible to prove that this change influenced Moses two generations later. In Akhenaten's reign the Egyptian vassals in Palestine, pressed both by the Hittites in the north and further incursions of Habiru from the deserts, appealed for help from the Egyptian king. Their anxieties can be followed in the correspondence, written on clay tablets in the cuneiform script, originally found at Amarna itself (see fig. 115), and in tablets of the same period from Ras Shamra.

After an interval of weakness Sethos I (whose father founded Dynasty

41

36. (*Below.*) *Tomb model of Brickmakers. The central man digs mud to be placed in the basket once held by the kneeling figure. The third man (left) presses the mud into a frame to form a brick, three rows of which lie before him.*
Beni Hassan. *c.* 2000 BC. Wood.   BM 63837.

37. (*Right.*) *Brick made of Nile mud and chopped straw, stamped with the name and title of Rameses II, possibly the pharaoh at the time of the oppression. See also figs. 36, 38.*
c. 1330 BC. Unbaked clay. 15 in. long.   BM 6020.

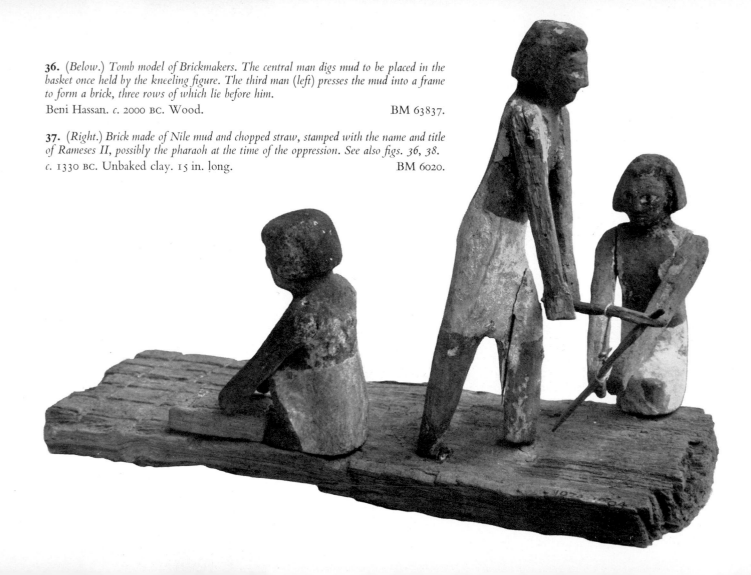

XIX) reigned *c.* 1304–1292 BC. He was the pharaoh 'who did not know of Joseph' (Exodus i. 8), and reconstruction work in Goshen commenced in his reign. The store-cities of Pithom (Tell Retabeh), excavated by Naville, and of Ra'amses were completed in the time of his son Rameses II (*c.* 1292–1226 BC). The latter city in 'the land of Ra'amses' (Genesis xlvii. 11) or 'the plain of Zoan' (Psalm lxxviii. 12, 43) has been plausibly identified with Tanis. No object of the preceding Dynasty XVIII has been found at either site during a series of excavations and this corroborates the dating of Exodus i. 11 in the reign of Rameses II (fig. 35). Some scholars place Ra'amses at nearby Qantir, but all agree that the revival of this capital four hundred years after its last use is a strong argument both for dating Joseph in the Hyksos period and for naming Rameses the Great as the pharaoh of the Exodus (Exodus xii. 40). From Ra'amses Rameses II sought to control his Asiatic Empire and from here his army and chariots marched into Palestine to fight the great battle with the Hittites at Kadesh illustrated on the walls of the king's temple (Ramesseum) at Thebes. Soon after (*c.* 1270), Rameses concluded a treaty with the Hittites and once again the Egyptian domination of Palestine grew weak.

The Hebrews who remained in Goshen were employed early in the reign on the great Delta reconstruction projects. Most of the unskilled worked as common labourers or brickmakers, a task illustrated by a tomb model of the Middle Kingdom (fig. 36) in which two men hack up the alluvium and place it in a basket (now missing) once held by the kneeling man. The third man on the left holds a hollow wooden frame into which the soil is pressed to form the brick. Three rows of bricks drying in the sun are represented. Unbaked bricks of this type stamped with the name and titles of Rameses II were found in the Delta area (fig. 37). The whole building operation supervised by taskmasters is graphically shown in a tomb painting (fig. 38). Other 'Asiatic' slaves were used in the quarries. Many more were employed in such mammoth tasks as the erection of

the 134 pillars of the great hypostyle hall at Karnak or of the thousand-ton statue cut from a single stone block for the Ramesseum in Western Thebes or of the ninety-foot colossus at Tanis. At Abu Simbel in distant Nubia the masons of Rameses II made a great temple by cutting the rock face to leave four sixty-foot high statues of the king at the entrance to the rockhewn halls which were decorated with painted frescoes.

The Egyptian religion of the time of Moses is well known. It was a mixture of popular respectability and elaborate funerary ritual with elementary crudities. Much thought and wealth were devoted to equipping the tomb and to the processions and feasts which accompanied burial.

The disasters which in Moses' day, as later, affected Egypt might well have been regarded as being directed against the various gods worshipped,

who were often thought to indwell animals (Exodus xii. 12). Thus in the plagues, the Nile which flows reddish in high summer was worshipped, as were deities symbolized by fishes, frogs and locusts. The plagues affected the earth (Seb), and the heavens (Nut) and sun (Rē' or Horus) were blotted out by a *khamsin* dust storm which can still last for several days in this area. The final plague has no natural explanation and was directed against the person of the 'divine' king. The faith of Moses, nurtured in the monotheism of Hebrew tradition, stands in clear contrast.

38. *Tomb painting showing men, including Syrian slaves, at work under a taskmaster 'making bricks to renew the workshop at Karnak' of the god Amun.*
Thebes (tomb of Rekh-mi-Re'). *c.* 1450 BC. 19 in. high.

From Lepsius, Denkmäler. III. 40.

The period covering the entry into Canaan has been much elucidated through archaeological research, although a number of problems as to the time and extent of the conquest still remain. The surveys of Transjordan by Glueck and Lankester Harding may explain why the Israelites under Moses avoided Edom and Moab. Before the thirteenth century these districts had been only sparsely inhabited, but now they were sufficiently settled and fortified to hamper any direct transit. Canaan, a fickle Egyptian province, was dominated by a few large city-states and a series of Egyptian military posts like Taanach and Bethshan which controlled the routes through Central Palestine. Jerusalem and other fortified towns were occupied by people of varied origins and semi-nomads occupied the intervening country. It is significant that the lightly armed Israelites avoided the most heavily defended localities. However, there is a clear break in many late Bronze Age sites throughout Palestine where a new and distinctive type of pottery, buildings and implements marks the succeeding Iron I phase (c. 1200 BC onwards).

Bethel, only indirectly mentioned in the biblical narrative of the conquest, was found in 1934 to have been violently destroyed by fire in the late Bronze Age as was Debir (Tell Beit Mirsim). Israeli excavators at Hazor, the northern Canaanite stronghold, attribute one level of destruction to Joshua's attack. Jericho (Tell es-Sultan), excavated by the British School of Archaeology in Jerusalem under Miss Kenyon from 1952 to 1958, probably fell at this time. The ruins of the contemporary towns show considerable denudation and very little remains. The fallen walls, once thought by Garstang to represent the destruction of the city by Joshua in 1407 BC, are now known to have been part of the fortifications of the city three hundred years earlier. At Lachish (Tell ed-Duweir) the widespread destruction of the period is further marked by an inscribed sherd dated in the early reign of Merneptah. This agrees with the earliest mention of Israel in extra-biblical texts (fig. 40) where Merneptah,

39. *(Left.) An example of Egyptian embalming. This mummy of the woman Katebet is covered with a mask, jewellery, pectorals and a shabti-figure. The Egyptians believed that the preservation of the body for the soul's use after death was a prime religious duty. The most expensive technique required the removal of organs easily susceptible to decay and steeping the body in salt, spices or natron for seventy days before swathing in bandages up to 600 yards long. A similar treatment was applied to the bodies of Jacob and Joseph (Genesis l. 2, 3, 26).*

Thebes. *c.* 1600–1200 BC. 6 ft. 2 in. long.

BM 6665.

40. *(Right.) Stele of the pharaoh Merneptah, celebrating his victory over the Libyans. The penultimate line contains the only direct reference to 'Israel' in inscriptions of this period.*

The king stands between the god Horus (right) and the goddess Mut (left) on either side of the god Amun, shown double, beneath the winged sun disk.

Thebes. 1224 BC. Limestone. 7 ft. 6 in. high.

Cairo Museum 34025.

41. (*Above.*) *Sphinx inscribed in a semitic language (Proto-Phoenician) written in an early alphabet based on Egyptian hieroglyphs (cf. fig. 42, col. ii). The goddess Ba'alat is named on the left side.*
Serabit al Hadim, Sinai. 15th century BC.
Red Sandstone. 9¾ in. long.　　BM 41748.

42. *Table showing the development of the alphabet from the pictographic scripts of Egypt and Sinai. The S. Arabian script (col. iv) preserves the formal style. The earlier Phoenician (Exodus period; col. v) and the Hebrew (col. vi; cf. Lachish Letters, fig. 64) are cursive forms.*

describing the Egyptian victories in Palestine, says that 'Canaan is despoiled ... Ashkelon captured ... Gezer taken ... Israel laid waste. Phoenicia (Khuru) has become as a widow for Egypt'. This implies that by 1222 BC the Israelites had already settled in the land and were themselves in difficulties.

Although all lines of evidence now point to the late thirteenth-century date for the Israelite entry into Canaan some problems still await further research for their solution. For example, Ai (Et-Tel) has been found to have lain since 2400 BC unoccupied except for a small and temporary Israelite settlement about 1000 BC. Many attempts have been made to explain this apparent discrepancy, none of them as yet very satisfactory.

The inclusion of accurate details in the Hebrew records of the sojourn in Egypt and its aftermath might well have resulted from the availability of written records. Moses, who was trained in all the wisdom of Egypt and received a court education, would have learned how to write both hieroglyphs (figs. 32, 40) and the flowing hieratic script, the business hand of Egypt (see fig. 31). He would learn how to use a reed pen and to use red ink for paragraph headings and how to set out work on a papyrus page or leather scroll. The conventions of fine literature and the approved methods of business and diplomacy, perhaps including the use of the cuneiform script which was still the international medium of communication, would have to be mastered. He would mix with high officials, noblemen, priests, military leaders and a varied society where he would not be the only man of foreign blood at court. Other Semites, and men from Libya and the East, held high rank in this general period, the most cosmopolitan in Egypt's history. They may well have brought knowledge of the alphabet of which the Proto-Phoenician or Hebrew script of Sinai was already in use (fig. 41), thus leading to an increasing use of this medium which was simpler than the more cumbrous cuneiform or hieroglyphic script (fig. 42; cf. fig. 22).

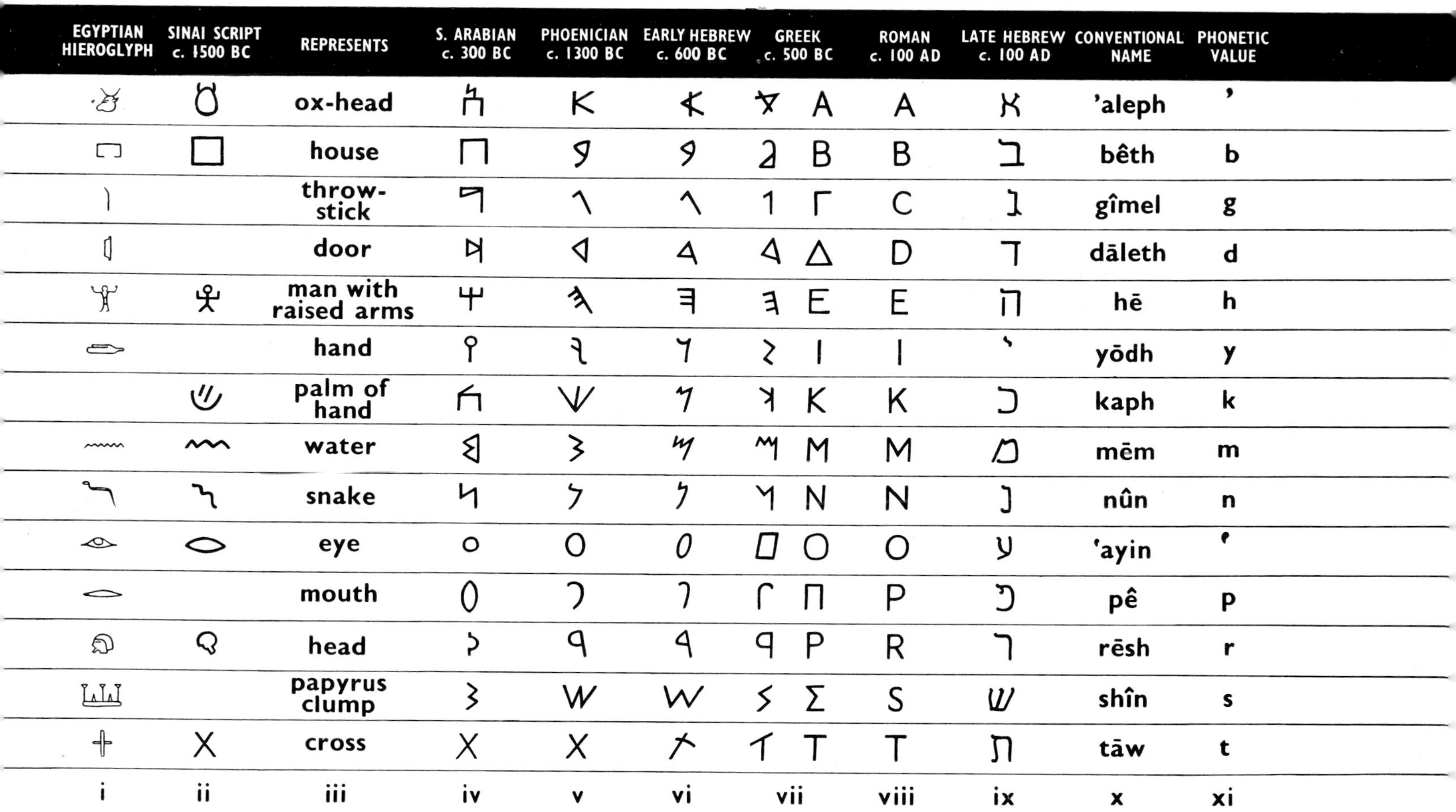

EGYPTIAN HIEROGLYPH	SINAI SCRIPT c. 1500 BC	REPRESENTS	S. ARABIAN c. 300 BC	PHOENICIAN c. 1300 BC	EARLY HEBREW c. 600 BC	GREEK c. 500 BC	ROMAN c. 100 AD	LATE HEBREW c. 100 AD	CONVENTIONAL NAME	PHONETIC VALUE
		ox-head				A	A	א	'aleph	'
		house				B	B	ב	bêth	b
		throw-stick				Γ	C	ג	gîmel	g
		door				Δ	D	ד	dāleth	d
		man with raised arms				E	E	ה	hē	h
		hand				I	I	י	yōdh	y
		palm of hand				K	K	כ	kaph	k
		water				M	M	מ	mēm	m
		snake				N	N	נ	nûn	n
		eye				O	O	ע	'ayin	'
		mouth				Π	P	פ	pê	p
		head				P	R	ר	rēsh	r
		papyrus clump				Σ	S	ש	shîn	s
		cross	X	X		T	T	ת	tāw	t
i	ii	iii	iv	v	vi	vii	viii	ix	x	xi

43. *Monument set up by Ashurnasirpal II, king of Assyria (884–859 BC), outside the entrance to the throne-room of his palace. It shows the king beneath the symbols of his tutelary deities. The text (154 lines) relates his conquests, building activities and the menu for the ten-day feast given to 69,574 persons at the dedication of the new palace.*

It has been suggested that this text gives an indication of the population of the city which was bounded by walls about four miles long (see map, fig. 46 on p. 52). In comparison the walls of Nineveh (fig. 45) enclose an area twice the size of Nimrud, so that the population of that city might well have been about 120,000 as claimed by Jonah (iv. 11).

Nimrud. 879 BC. Sandstone. 4 ft. 2 in. high. Mosul Museum.

CHAPTER IV

IN THE DAYS OF THE KINGS

The Israelites in Palestine were destined to face the military forces of the Assyrian Empire; but except for some raids into Syria by Tiglath-pileser I (*c.* 1100 BC) it was not until the ninth century, in the reign of Ashurnasirpal II, that the Assyrian armies began a systematic assault on the west. This king re-established the capital at Kalhu (modern Nimrud, the Calah of Genesis x. 11), where the British School of Archaeology in Iraq has from 1949 to 1958 been uncovering many richly equipped palaces and buildings. In 1951 a monument was discovered near the gateway of the royal palace (fig. 43). On this Ashurnasirpal described his campaigns and building activities and the ten-day feast which marked the opening of the city in 879 BC. The work of rebuilding and dragging into position the massive stone colossi which guarded the gateways of the citadel, palaces and temples (fig. 44) had been done by captives and slaves, some from the west, who were thereafter settled in as the new population.

There is increasing evidence that some of the cities at this time were thickly populated. Jonah (iv. 11) claimed to have preached to 120,000 persons 'who did not know right from wrong', living within the eight-mile circuit of the outer walls of Nineveh (see fig. 45). Since the inscription from Nimrud, twenty-two miles to the south, shows that about 60,000

44. *Human-headed winged bull, guarding the gateway to the palace of Ashurnasirpal II, king of Assyria (see also fig. 43). Similar composite creatures, called* kurubu, *were the original of the biblical cherubim (cf. fig. 114).*

Nimrud. 879 BC. Gypsum. 10 ft. 5 in. high. BM 118872.

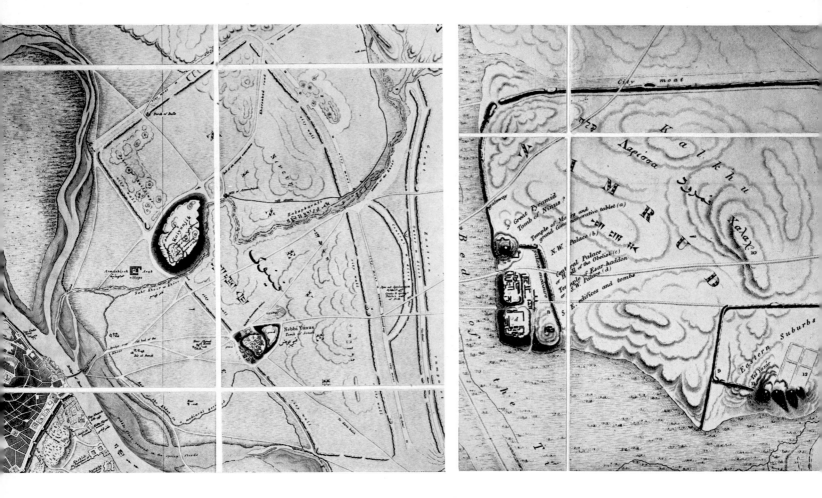

people were housed within its walls, measuring four and a quarter miles in circuit (fig. 46), Jonah's claim is not so anomalous as has been supposed.

But the early Israelite settlers in Canaan had to face other foes, in particular the Philistines, a seafaring people from Anatolia who were active in the eastern Mediterranean as early as *c.* 1500 BC, though their presence at Gezer and Tell Qasileh near the coast is not evidenced until three centuries later. By 1050 BC they had overrun Debir, Beth-zur and Shiloh, continuing the Israelitic settlement to the hills. Their supremacy was based on their exclusive possession of the technique of iron-working (1 Samuel xiii. 19-22). Their resulting military superiority was only broken by David, who may perhaps be the ruler who strengthened the walls of Debir and Bethshemesh against the Philistines. Only a single iron implement was found in Saul's simple palace at Gibeah before the debris shows that it, too, fell to the Philistine invaders. Thereafter, although the standard of Israelite culture improves, archaeology reveals little of David's reign, unless the defences of Ophel, part of the new capital of the 'city of David', can be attributed to him.

The continuing weakness of the great powers, Egypt and Assyria, and the preoccupation of Sidon and the ports with overseas trade left David free to move successfully against the Philistines, Aramaeans, Edom and Moab. The long reign of his successor Solomon (*c.* 961-922) was one of the greatest material advance. He was able to concentrate on the economic development of the state. At Ezion-geber (Tell el-Kheleifeh, 1 Kings

45, 46. (*Left.*) *Maps of Nineveh and Nimrud drawn by Felix Jones in 1856. Scale 1½ and 3 inches to the mile respectively.*

47. *View of the ruins, showing roof-pillars probably used as hitching-posts for horses, at Solomon's store-city of Megiddo (1 Kings ix. 15, 19). Above, the reconstruction of the stables which held twenty-four horses. Two areas of similar buildings had an estimated capacity of 930 horses.*

Megiddo C. *c.* 900 BC.   Oriental Institute, Chicago, Expedition 1925-39.

ix. 26) he built a large copper smelting plant, fed from quarries south of the Dead Sea, and a harbour. A potsherd inscribed 'from Ophir', found at Tell Qasileh, shows that he traded actively with distant places, by sea and by camel caravan. By acting as a middleman, trading horses from Cilicia (Kue, so 1 Kings x. 28-29) and chariots from Egypt, Solomon quickly augmented the national resources. At Megiddo, where, like Hazor and Gezer, identical Solomonic gateways and buildings are now known, there was stabling for more than nine hundred horses (fig. 47). Beth-shemesh and Lachish were rebuilt as district centres for the receipt and storage of taxes paid in kind.

Solomon dedicated part of his new wealth to the construction of the Temple at Jerusalem. His Phoenician master-craftsmen followed the general plan of earlier Canaanite temples such as that found at Hazor in 1957 and resembling a similar smaller temple at Tell Tainat (Syria) dated in the following century. Entry was up a flight of stairs between two pillars, through a door leading directly into a large hall (*hekal*) and thence directly into a small inner and dimly lit sanctuary (*debir*). The use of wood courses between the stonework (1 Kings vi. 36) is known from excavations at Ras Shamra and Alalah. The *cherubim*, or pair of winged human-headed lions (cf. fig. 44), appear on ivories from Megiddo as do some of the other decorative motifs in the Temple (palm trees and lotus flowers). Some of the temple furniture, lavers, censers and instruments of sacrifice, are known from Palestinian, Syrian and Assyrian sites. This period was undoubtedly one of literary activity, but the only native inscription of the reign is the Gezer Calendar, a school exercise or mnemonic ditty in verse for children describing the seasons. The script

48. *Inscription of Mesha, king of Moab, recording his successful revolt after the death of Ahab (2 Kings i. 1, iii. 4, 5). He lists the villages taken from Israel by the help of the Moabite god Chemosh (2 Kings xxiii. 13, etc.).*

Dhiban. *c.* 830 BC. Black basalt. 3 ft. 3 in. high.   Louvre AO 5066.

was similar to that of the Moabite stone (fig. 48).

When Solomon died, the monarchy was weakened by a resurgence of tribal factions and Jeroboam's appeal for help to Egypt led to the invasion by Shishak (Sheshonq I), founder of the Bubastite 22nd Dynasty. He invaded Judah, destroying Debir and Bethshemesh, and, according to I Kings xiv. 25-26 and 2 Chronicles xii. 2-4, sacked Jerusalem and penetrated not only to Israel, where one of his inscribed stelae was found at Megiddo, but also to Edom, Phoenicia and Syria. These operations are known from a list of more than a hundred and fifty towns, which included a number in Judah and Israel known from the Bible, inscribed on the wall of the Amun temple at Karnak. The incomplete statue of the king shows him smiting Hebrew captives before Amen-Re', king of the gods. The dynasty of Sheshonq lived for some decades on the wealth and trade captured from Palestine. The fine pair of bracelets inscribed with the name of Shishak were dedicated by him about 935 BC (fig. 49).

Archaeological evidence for the divided monarchy is found in Jeroboam's reconstruction work at Shechem (I Kings xii. 25) and the fortifications of Gibeah, Bethel and Tell en-Nasbeh (probably Mizpah), which emphasize the ferocity of the internal strife between Judah and Israel (I Kings xv. 16-22). The current excavations by De Vaux at Tell el Far'ah, the site of Tirzah, the former capital of Israel, show that the site was abandoned in favour of Samaria where excavations in 1908-10 and 1932-35 uncovered successive occupation levels. The original buildings of Omri-Ahab included the palace and furniture decorated with ivories (I Kings xxii. 39; Amos vi. 4) and the pool where Ahab's chariot was washed down (I Kings xxii. 38). Omri's influence is to be seen in the inscription of Mesha of Moab (fig. 48) who tells how Israel reconquered part of his territory and resettled it with Israelites. Moab regained her independence after the death of Ahab.

The first firm chronological link in the contacts between Assyria and

49. *Pair of bracelets made for the prince Nemareth by his father Sheshonq I, the Egyptian king Shishak who raided Jerusalem (1 Kings xiv. 25). The design shows the infant god Harpocrates emerging from a lotus.*

c. 940 BC (XIIth Dynasty). Gold and lapis lazuli. 2¾ in. high.   BM 14594-5.

Israel is given in the description by Shalmaneser III of the battle of Qarqar on the Orontes in 853 BC. In the coalitions of his opponents under Irhuleni (Benhadad) of Hamath he lists '200 chariots and 10,000 men of Ahab, the Israelite'. Shalmaneser also claimed the defeat of Hazael of Damascus near Mt. Hermon, called Shenir as in Deuteronomy iii. 9, and henceforward Israel dwelt under the shadow of Assyria's increasing military might.

The temporary league between Israel and Syria in face of the Assyrian threat soon broke up and Jehu resumed the former hostility against Damascus. In 841 BC Jehu brought tribute to Shalmaneser and this is illustrated on that king's 'Black obelisk' in the British Museum (figs. 3, 50). In the inscription, above the only contemporary portrait of a king of Israel named in the Old Testament, Jehu is called 'Son of Omri' which can mean either 'descendant of', or 'of the Dynasty of' Omri, or 'citizen of (Beth-) Omri', for Samaria was called Bit-Humri by the Assyrians just as Damascus was sometimes referred to as Bit-Hazaili. The four sides of the obelisk show Israelites bearing gifts which are described as 'the tribute of Jehu, son of Omri. Silver, gold, a golden bowl, a golden vase, golden cups, golden buckets, tin and royal staff and *puruhati*—fruits' (fig. 51). This incident is not mentioned in the Bible, but may have been part of a policy to gain Assyrian support against Hazael. If this were so it was unsuccessful, for internal revolts in Assyria during the early co-regency of Adad-nirari III and his mother Sammuramat (Semiramis) meant that, apart from one raid to the west, the Assyrians did not venture there again until after Jehu's death.

50. (*Left.*) *One side of the black obelisk of Shalmaneser III (see also fig. 3), showing thirteen Israelites wearing long garments covered with fringed cloaks, pointed soft caps and sandals with upturned toes. They carry the tribute described, in the text above the second register from the top, as 'silver, gold, golden bowls, vase, vessels and buckets, (a block of) tin, a royal staff and* puruhati—fruits'. *The latter are seen carried on a tray.* Nimrud. 841 BC. Limestone. 6 ft. 6 in. high.   BM 118885.

51. (*Right.*) *A near view of the front panel of the same monument showing 'Jehu, son of Omri' bowing before the Assyrian king in the presence of an Assyrian officer and attendants. This is the only contemporary representation of any Israelite king. His action is not mentioned, but is possibly implied, in the Old Testament history.*

52. *A scaraboid-shaped stamp seal, engraved with a roaring lion, frequently used as the symbol for Judah, and the Egyptian ankh, symbol of life. The style points to the mixed cultural influences on Palestine at the time. The seal is inscribed lshm' 'bdyrbm, 'belonging to Shema', servant of Jeroboam', probably Jeroboam II (785–743 BC). On such seals the term 'servant' designates 'minister', as on the seal of Jaazaniah (2 Kings xxv. 23) found at Tell en-Nasbeh. In Palestine, under Egyptian influence, the stamp seal was more commonly used than the cylinder seal. The latter continued in use in Mesopotamia until the Persian period. (See fig. 71.)*

Megiddo. 8th century BC. Jasper. 1½ in. long. Istanbul Museum.

In the reign of Joahaz the Aramaeans reduced Israel and Phoenicia to dependent states and Jehoash of Judah to a tribute-paying vassal. When Adad-nirari reasserted his Assyrian domination over Syria in 802 BC Israel was able to recover much of her lost territory in wars with Benhadad, son of Hazael, and even to make Judah a vassal of Israel. Under Jeroboam II (*c.* 786–746 BC) the northern kingdom flourished. Inscribed sherds or dockets, dated between 778 and 770 BC, were found in the ruins of Samaria in 1910 and 1932. The city (levels IV-VI) was an active trading and administrative centre, exporting and importing wine. The personal names on the dockets show that half as many persons had names with the element Ba'al as had the divine name Yahweh and this may be indicative of the religious life of the times. Many bore names similar to those of the tribe of Manasseh, the former inhabitants of the area (Numbers xxvi. 29-33; I Chronicles vii. 14-19). These brief inscriptions also illustrate the northern dialects of biblical Hebrew. Among the seals of this reign is a fine specimen found at Megiddo in 1904 inscribed 'belonging to Shema', the servant of Jeroboam' (fig. 52).

Azariah (Uzziah) of Judah is mentioned in the annals of Tiglath-pileser III, king of Assyria (745-727 BC), who is also called by his native name Pul(u) in 2 Kings xv. 19 and in Babylonian texts (see fig. 59). The prosperity of Uzziah's reign can be seen in building activity in the Negeb and his revival of the port of Elath (formerly Ezion-geber). At this site the inscribed seal of Jotham, his son and co-regent, was discovered. Seals of two officials of this period are known, Abiyau (Abiah) and Shebanyau (Shebnaiah), both inscribed 'servant of Uzziyau (Uzziah)'.

Meanwhile, in the north, Tiglath-pileser subdued Syria in a series of campaigns during which Israel remained independent only by paying tribute. Menahem, named in the Assyrian texts, raised the dues by a tax equivalent to the current price of a slave on each Israelite noble (2 Kings xv. 20). Nevertheless, soon afterwards, the Assyrian claims to have

'marched through the borders of Israel' perhaps at the request of Ahaz (called (Jeho)ahaz by the Assyrians) who paid tribute in 734 BC. The Assyrian annals tell how Hoshea was replaced by Pekah as king of Israel. When the latter revolted in league with Damascus, the Assyrian armies returned and destroyed Damascus, Megiddo (level III) and Hazor. A solitary inscribed sherd bearing the king's name (*pqh*) found at Hazor is witness to his end.

In 721 BC the resistance of Israel was finally crushed by the capture of Samaria by Sargon II, who took over the siege operations begun by his father, Shalmaneser V, three years before (2 Kings xvii. 1-6). Sargon is frequently depicted on the wall reliefs of his palace at Khorsabad, now in Chicago, Paris and London (see fig. 2). Among the booty he took 'the

53. *The lintel of a tomb prepared for (Shebna)-yahu, a royal steward called 'he who is over the house' (cf. the use of this title on the seal of Gedaliah; fig. 65). The name Shebna, or Shebnaiah, is found on several Palestinian seals. This tomb was conspicuously set in a necropolis occupied by those of high rank, and the text, the third longest monumental inscription in archaic Hebrew (cf. figs. 48, 56), supports the opinion that this is the tomb of the Shebna rebuked by Isaiah (xxii. 15-16).*

Siloam (Jerusalem). 7th century BC. Limestone. 7 ft. 3 in. long. BM 125205.

59

gods in whom they (Israel) trusted', a clear allusion to the polytheism of Israel so strongly condemned by the prophets. The same prism text, found at Nimrud in 1952, also describes the desolation of Babylon in terms closely paralleled in Isaiah xiii. Sargon deported some of the prisoners from Samaria to Gozan or Guzana (Tell Halaf) where excavations have shown evidence of the presence of Jewish exiles. He also records the resettlement of the city by peoples drawn from distant parts of his empire (so 2 Kings xvii. 24). The absorption of Israel into the Assyrian provincial system meant that from this time Judah had to face Assyria alone.

The historical background of the prophecies of Isaiah is provided by a number of contemporary records. One inscription, on a rock lintel from a tomb (fig. 53), was read by Avigad in 1953: 'This is the (the sepulchre of Shebna)yahu who is over the house. There is no silver or gold here, but only (his bones) and the bones of his slave-wife with him. Cursed be the man who breaks this open.'

The restoration of the name, the same as Shebna, is based on his office. 'He who is over the house', i.e. 'palace-governor', occurs on a number of seals (cf. fig. 65). An official of this name and office was rebuked by Isaiah for building a pretentious tomb (Isaiah xxii. 15-16).

Sennacherib, son of Sargon, attacked Judah in 701 BC, besieged Hezekiah in Jerusalem and laid waste a number of towns, including Debir and Lachish (2 Kings xviii. 17, xix. 8), perhaps in an attempt to thwart the arrival of any Egyptian aid for the besieged capital. Bas-reliefs from the walls of Sennacherib's palace at Nineveh show the siege-engines moving up ramps to breach the walls of Lachish (see fig. 57). Refugees pour out

54. *Hexagonal clay prism inscribed with the details of eight campaigns by Sennacherib, king of Assyria, 705-681 BC. The operations against Merodach-Baladan in Babylon and his invasion of Palestine in 701 BC, when he besieged 'Hezekiah the Judaean' in Jerusalem, are given. He also claims to have received tribute as recorded in 2 Kings xviii. 13-16.* Nineveh. 686 BC. 15 in. high.   BM 91032 (Taylor Prism).

of the burning city and 'prisoners (and booty) from Lachish pass in review before Sennacherib, king of the world, king of Assyria, seated on his portable throne'—so runs the cuneiform caption. This is the earliest portrait of Judaeans who, as prisoners, are shown on other sculptures of this king's reign at work building his palace and moving huge, half-cut bull-colossi into position. Some Judaeans may be identified among the royal body-guard in later years. The details of the siege as shown on the relief were remarkably confirmed by the Wellcome-Marston expedition to Lachish (Tell ed-Duweir) in 1932-1938. The ruins of the city, one of the largest in Palestine, cover eighteen acres. The destruction of level III is marked by fire and the walls by the main gate at the south-west show repairs where the breach was made. Part of the ramp, slingstones, arrowheads, scale armour and even the crest of the helmet of one Assyrian attacker mark the point of the final attack. A common grave filled with 1,500 bodies may represent the clearance of the site following the siege.

There is much controversy over the date of the siege of Jerusalem itself. Albright maintains that the biblical history is a conflation of the accounts of two invasions of Judah. He argues that one attack in 701 BC was bought off by Hezekiah paying tribute, and the Assyrians retreated as described in 2 Kings xix. 35, 36. The other followed a revolt by Judah after the accession of Tirhakah of Egypt which, according to Albright, took place in 689 BC and therefore his intervention must have occurred between that date and Hezekiah's death in 686 BC. But the theory of a single-campaign in 701 BC is supported by many scholars. The order of events in Egypt, Assyria and Judah is not so precisely known as to be decisive proof of the contrary view. Sennacherib in his own account of a single operation claims to have 'shut up Hezekiah, the Judaean, in his royal city like a bird in a cage' (fig. 54). He makes no claim to the capture of the city and this may be taken as an indication that he withdrew without successfully concluding the siege. The assassination of Sennacherib in 681 BC is mentioned in

55. *The Siloam tunnel, over 500 yards long, cut by Hezekiah to bring water into Jerusalem from a spring outside the city (2 Kings xx. 20). See also fig. 56.*

Jerusalem. Average height 5 ft.
Photo: Palestine Archaeological Museum.

56. (*Above.*) *The inscription found in the Siloam tunnel (fig. 55) describing how the miners excavating the water conduit from above and below finally met in the centre. The scripts in archaic Hebrew supports a date in Hezekiah's reign (cf. figs. 48, 53).*
Jerusalem. *c.* 710 BC. 2 ft. 6 in. long.   Istanbul Museum.

57. (*Right.*) *Relief showing 'Sennacherib, king of Assyria, sitting upon his throne while the spoil from the city of Lachish passed before him'. So runs the cuneiform inscription above him. Other reliefs show the capture of Lachish in 701 BC (2 Kings xviii. 13, 17).*
Nineveh. *c.* 690 BC. Gypsum. 6 ft. high.   BM 124911.

58. *The figure of 'Tirhakah, king of Ethiopia', the ally of Hezekiah (2 Kings xix. 9), placed beneath the protection of the god Amun, shown as a colossal recumbant ram. The inscription on the plinth describes the Nubian pharaoh Taharqa, 'who fully satisfies the heart of his father Amun'.* Karnak. *c.* 675 BC. Grey granite. 2 ft. 1 in. high. BM 1779.

Assyrian texts and in 1 Kings xix. 37, neither of which necessarily implies that his death followed immediately after his return from the west.

Hezekiah's ability to withstand the Assyrians has been ascribed to his foresight in constructing new defences and a tunnel to bring water from Siloam into the city in time of siege (2 Kings xx. 20; 2 Chronicles xxxii. 30). This tunnel (fig. 55) is thought by some to be the same as that climbed by David's troops when the city was first captured (2 Samuel v. 8), but other aqueducts are known. The tunnel, first mentioned in 1838 by the American explorer Robinson, was found in 1880 to have been inscribed on one wall. The inscription (fig. 56) is the second longest monumental text in early Hebrew and is important for the study of the script. The text may be rendered:

'. . . was being dug out. It was cut in the following manner. . . . axes, each man towards his fellow and while there were still three cubits to be cut, the voice of one man calling to the other was heard showing that he was deviating to the right. When the tunnel was driven through, the excavators met man to man, axe against axe, and the water flowed for 1,200 cubits from the spring to the reservoir. The height of the rock above the heads of the excavators was 100 cubits.'

Under Esarhaddon (681-669 BC) the Assyrian empire included lower Egypt where he had made the Ethiopian king Tirhakah a vassal. Statues of this king have been found at Nineveh and he is shown as a captive on Esarhaddon's victory stele set up at Senjirli. A figure of the pharaoh set up in the temple of Amun at Kawa in 673 is now in the British Museum (fig. 58).

Many texts of the final decades of the great Assyrian empire have been recovered. At this time the scribes wrote the cuneiform script both on clay tablets and on writing boards, the earliest of which, dated about 711 BC, was found in a well at Nimrud. The reliefs also show scribes

59. *Tiglath-pileser III, king of Assyria, 745–727 BC, also known by his native name Pul(u) in Babylonian texts (2 Kings xv. 19; 1 Chronicles v. 26). He stands in his war chariot, together with a driver and 'third man', sometimes translated 'captain' (2 Kings x. 25, xv. 25, etc.).*

In his royal annals Tiglath-pileser makes a number of direct references to Old Testament characters, naming Azariah (Azriau) of Judah, Menahem (Menihimme) of Samaria and (Jeho)ahaz (Iauhazi) who paid him tribute. He claims to have replaced Pekah (Paqaha) by Hoshea (Ausi') on the throne of Israel during his campaigns in Syria and Palestine in 734–732 BC.

Nimrud. *c.* 740 BC. Gypsum. 2 ft. 2½ in. high.
BM 118908.

writing in Aramaic on papyrus or leather scrolls (fig. 60). One sherd found at Nimrud in 1955 was inscribed with a list of Hebrew names, perhaps captives from the time of Esarhaddon. The various types of literature are well known from the royal library of Nineveh, collected by Ashurbanipal (669–*c.* 631 BC) and now in the British Museum. Among them are detailed works on medicine, mathematics, astronomy, geology and lexicography, and copies of earlier texts collected from temples throughout the land.

One of the most interesting tablets recently discovered is a treaty or list of covenant terms drawn up by Esarhaddon in 672 BC. This tablet gives in great detail the stipulations imposed upon his subjects, among whom he elsewhere lists 'Manasseh (*Menasi*), king of Judah'. The vassal swore to treat the principal Assyrian god, Ashur, as his own god, just as 2 Kings xvi. 10 implies Ahaz had done in the days of Tiglath-pileser III. The seal of the god Ashur, the first such seal known, is seen on the left of fig. 61. All vassals swore to keep the covenant which was 'for ever' and to repeat it to succeeding generations. The clauses are all written as direct speech in the form 'Thou shalt ... thou shalt not. ...'. They required a spoken assent, and are followed by curses, a number of which are similar to those of the earlier Hebrew covenants (Deuteronomy xxviii; Joshua xxiv). In contrast to the Hebrew covenant, witnessed by the God of Israel alone and drawn up with a primarily spiritual purpose, this 'covenant' bears a long list of deities as witnesses, and seeks to provide a stable succession to the throne. As so often happens, history shows that the oaths were soon violated.

61. *A vassal-treaty or covenant tablet showing two of the three seals. On the left, but central on the document, is the unique seal of the god Ashur. Israelite and Judaean kings who submitted to Assyria would have had to subscribe to terms similar to those dictated on this tablet (see above).*

Nimrud. 672 BC. Rt. seal 4 in. high.   Iraq Museum.

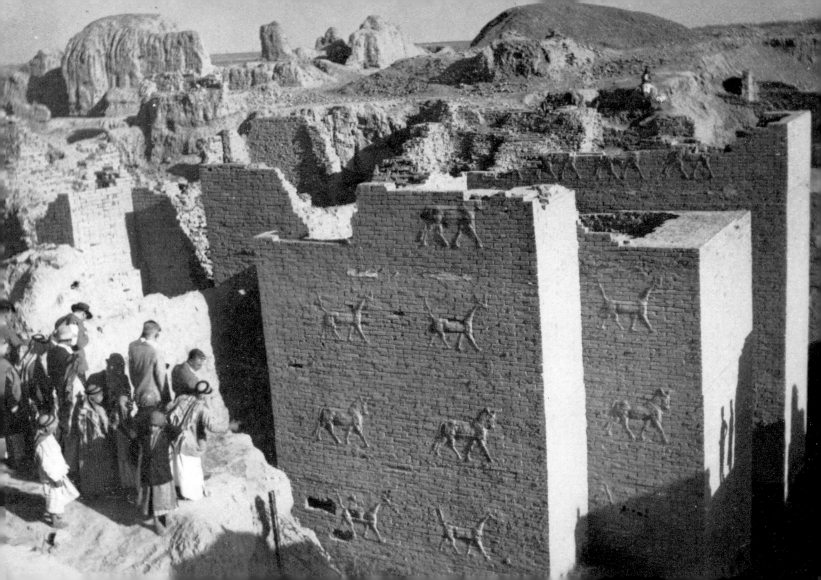

CHAPTER V

THE EXILE AND AFTER

The events which led to the captivity of the Jews in Babylon (see fig. 69) were, until recently, known only from the Old Testament and a few references in Josephus and Herodotus. The publication in 1956 of additional tablets of the contemporary Babylonian Chronicle enables a full picture of the major historical episodes to be given from this unique and reliable source. After recounting the fall of Nineveh to the Babylonians and Medes in August 612 BC it traces the relations between Necho II of Egypt and Nabopolassar of Babylon until the Battle of Carchemish in 605 BC. Nebuchadrezzar, at that time crown prince, claimed to have conquered the whole of Syro-Palestine as implied by 2 Kings xxiv. 7 and, immediately after his accession on 6th September 605 BC, to have received a tribute from 'all the kings of Hatti (Syro-Palestine) who came before him' in 604. Among those who submitted at this time was Jehoiakim who remained loyal until after the defeat of the Babylonians by the Egyptians in a great battle in 601 BC, known only from this Chronicle. The inevitable Babylonian revenge came after raids on the Arabs of Kedar as described by Jeremiah (xlix. 28-33). The Chronicle (fig. 63) records that 'In the seventh year (of Nebuchadrezzar) in the month of Kislev, the Babylonian king mustered his troops and, having

62. (*Left.*) *General view of the ruins of the Ishtar gate at Babylon (cf. figs. 67, 68).*

63. (*Above.*) *The Babylonian Chronicle for 605-594 BC. The events described include the Battle of Carchemish and the accession of Nebuchadrezzar II in 605 BC. The fifth paragraph relates the capture of Jerusalem on March 16th, 597 BC, the appointment of Zedekiah as king and the removal of Jehoiachin and other prisoners to exile in Babylonia. See also fig. 69 and p. 73.*

6th century BC. 3¼ in. high.   BM 21946.

marched to the land of Hatti, besieged the city of Judah. On the second day of the month Adar he captured the city and seized the king. He set up in it a king after his heart and having received its heavy tribute sent (them) off to Babylon.' Compare with this 2 Kings xxiv. 10-17.

This is a clear reference to the capture of Jehoiachin and to the plundering of the temple and city. The king chosen to succeed was Zedekiah, and the exiles despatched to Babylon a few days later 'at the turn of the year' (2 Chronicles xxxvi. 10) included the royal family. The date (16th March 597 BC) provides a firm point in both biblical and Babylonian chronology. When Zedekiah revolted against his overlord in 589, he and Jeremiah would well know that the Babylonian armies would inevitably sack the city for breaking the vassal-treaty to which he had sworn (see p. 66). The same fate had befallen Ashkelon in 604 BC, despite the city's appeal for help from Egypt in a papyrus letter written in Aramaic found at Saqqarah. The impact of that event may have been the cause of the fast proclaimed in Jeremiah xxxvi. 1-9. Prisoners from Jerusalem, as from Ashkelon, were employed on the lavish building projects of Nebuchadrezzar who was then engaged in embellishing his great capital city and adding to the fortifications (fig. 66).

The severe nature of the final siege of Jerusalem in 589-587 BC is shown by the utter devastation of Judah which took place at this time. In the debris of the guardroom by the city gate of Lachish eighteen inscribed potsherds were found. Some, invoking the name of Y(a)hw(e)h, mention restriction of movement and the 'princes who weaken the hands', perhaps the very opponents of Jeremiah. The majority were messages passing between Hosha 'yahu, the commander of an outpost, and Ya'ush, military

64. *Part of the correspondence, in Hebrew on potsherds, between Lachish and an outpost during the Babylonian invasion of Judah in 589-587 BC.*
Lachish. *c.* 588 BC. Approx. $\frac{1}{3}$ size.   Palestine Archaeological Museum.

65. *Impression made by a scaraboid seal. Inscribed* lgdlyh ashr 'lhbyt, *'belonging to Gedaliah who is over the house'. This may well be the Gedaliah who was made governor of Judah by the Babylonians in 583 BC (2 Kings xxv. 23).*
Lachish, 6th century BC. Twice actual size.

66. (*Right.*) *Brick inscribed with the name and titles of Nebuchadrezzar II, king of Babylonia, 605-562 BC, and recording his restoration of the temples of the gods Marduk (Merodach) and Nabu (Nebo), Esagila and Ezida, at Babylon.*
Babylon. 6th century BC. Approx. 12½ in. square. BM 90081.

67, 68. *A reconstruction (left) of the Ishtar gate (cf. fig. 62) showing the decoration of alternating rows of bulls and serpent-dragons. These composite creatures (mushrussu) had the head of a serpent, a lion's body and hind claws of an eagle (see above).*

Babylon. 605-562 BC. 48 ft. high.

Berlin Museum.

69. *(Right.) List of rations given to prisoners held at Babylon. 'Jehoiachin, King of Judah' and his sons are named among the recipients.*

Babylon. 593 BC. Clay. $3\frac{3}{4}$ in. wide.

Berlin Museum (VAT 16378).

governor of Lachish. Letter No. IV (fig. 64) ends 'and let my lord know that we are waiting for the fire-signals of Lachish according to the indications which my lord has given, because we cannot see (the fire-signals of) Azekah'. Jeremiah (vi. 1, xxxiv. 7) mentions 'fire-signals' and tells how Lachish and Azekah were focal points in the Babylonian campaign. Lachish, Bethshemesh and Debir, which showed signs of increasing poverty after the war of 597 BC, now fell, their gates and fortifications were pulled down, the buildings set on fire and the sites, as in many other places in Judah, were abandoned or only sparsely inhabited thereafter. No town in Judah has been found to have been continuously occupied throughout the exilic period. In contrast, towns in the south (Negeb) and to the north of the border (Bethel), and in the Babylonian province of Samaria, have been found undestroyed at this critical time. A seal-impression inscribed 'Gedaliah who is over the house', perhaps the mayor who was later appointed Prime Minister and subsequently murdered (2 Kings xxv. 22-26), was found in the ruins of Lachish (fig. 65) and another inscribed with the name of 'Jaazaniah, servant of the king' at Tell en-Nasbeh.

A number of tablets were found in an administrative building at Babylon near the Ishtar gate (figs. 67, 68; see also fig. 62). Some of these list the foreign prisoners who received rations of oil and barley from the royal storehouses and are dated between 595 and 570 BC. Among them Jehoiachin (Yaukin), his five sons and eight other Judaeans are named together with other royalty and craftsmen from places in Egypt, Philistia (Ashkelon), Phoenicia, Syria, Cilicia, Lydia, Elam, Media and Persia, some of which are mentioned in the prophecies of Jeremiah. Jehoiachin, held as a hostage, was still called 'king of Judah' (fig. 69). His royal estates in Judah continued to be managed, at least between 597 and 587, by 'Eliakim, steward of Jehoiachin', impressions of whose seal were found at Debir and Bethshemesh.

The period of the exile in Palestine and Babylon remains obscure.

70. *Cylinder of Cyrus, king of Babylonia 538-529 BC, recording his capture of Babylon without a battle. He states that he remedied the evil done by his predecessors by sending prisoners from Babylonia back to their own lands. He aided the restoration of their temples and returned their gods. This edict would have included the Jews (cf. Ezra i.).*

Babylon. 536 BC. Baked clay. 9 in. long.   BM 90920.

Many Neo-Babylonian administrative tablets and a few building inscriptions show that after the reign of Nebuchadrezzar there was a marked decline in the economy and an increasing weakness both military and political. It was a period without literary distinction, though the increasing use of fragile papyri inscribed in Aramaic may account for the absence of literary works. The attempted religious reforms of Nabonidus (556-539 BC) led to his exile in Tema' in Arabia for ten years. He left the government in the hands of his son and co-regent Belshazzar, whose activities are known from other tablets. A stele from Harran, published by C. J. Gadd in 1958, describes the flight and exile of Nabonidus. His return in 546 BC was welcomed, he claims, by 'the king of the Medes', who at this time must have been Cyrus. Nevertheless, the Babylonian Chronicle for 538 BC graphically describes the capture of Babylon by the army of Cyrus. The identity of 'Darius the Mede' remains an open question, and must await further evidence, probably from some archaeological discovery. Since the recently discovered Harran text it has been suggested that this was another throne-name of Cyrus himself or of Gubaru, a local provincial governor.

The arrival of Cyrus brought peace and prosperity to the former Babylonian realm. He made few innovations and was soon able to claim in Babylon that he had returned to their former places the images of gods brought into Babylon (see fig. 70), that he had restored their temples and had sent prisoners back to their own lands. The return of the Jews to Judah is to be seen in the sparse traces of resettlement found at Gezer, Lachish, Bethel, Gibeah and Beth-zur.

The Persian government over the west was strengthened under Darius I (521-486 BC) and at this time Judah was part of the fifth satrapy comprising Syria-Palestine ('Transpotamia'). The satrapies were linked by couriers. Aramaic was increasingly used throughout the empire although the cuneiform script was still used for many Babylonian texts.

71. *Cylinder seal and impression showing Darius I, king of Babylon, hunting. The winged-disk emblem of Ahuramazda, the national god of ancient Persia, is above him. The trilingual inscription gives his name and title ('The Great King') in Old Persian, Elamite and Babylonian cuneiform (cf. fig. 109).*
Thebes. 521-486 BC. Agate. $1\frac{4}{5}$ in. high.
BM 89132.

72. (*Above.*) *A large golden bowl with flutes and bosses inscribed with the name of Darius. The style is typical of metal vessels found at this period in Palestine and throughout the ancient Near East.*

Hamadan. 5th century BC. 8¼ in. diameter.
Metropolitan Museum, New York.

73. (*Right.*) *Darius sits on his throne holding a long sceptre. His son, crown prince Xerxes, stands behind him while he receives a Median.*

Persepolis treasury. 521–486 BC. Limestone.
8 ft. high. Teheran.

Outside the Old Testament and the Babylonian references to Jehoiachin, the only information we have regarding the life of the Jews in exile dates from the fifth century. Thirty-eight Hebrew names, some of them compounded with the divine element Yau, occur on 730 account tablets belonging to Murashu and sons, a family of bankers at Nippur (Babylonia) in 464–404 BC (in the reign Artaxerxes I—Darius II). Similar names are found among the papyri from Elephantine (Yeb) in Upper Egypt. A Jewish garrison built a temple there about 525 BC, soon after Jeremiah had migrated into Egypt. The finds include a copy of an Edict of Darius II concerning the observance of the Passover in 419 BC. In 408 BC the elders petitioned Bagoi, the Persian governor of Judah, for permission to rebuild their temple which had been destroyed during riots three years earlier while Arsham, the Persian governor of Egypt, had been on leave. The letter mentions that a previous appeal to Johanan the high priest (cf. Nehemiah xii. 22-23) had not been answered. Having failed to interest the orthodox party, they next wrote to the rival group, under the sons of Sanballat, governor of Samaria, Nehemiah's opponent. This only brought advice to apply direct to Arsham, and this they did, stating that no animal sacrifices were involved. An ally of Sanballat, Geshem (called Gashmu, or Gusham) the Arab (Nehemiah ii. 19), is named in both Babylonian and Arabian texts of this century as the king of Kedar. The family of Tobiah of Amnon can be traced through a number of inscriptions found in Jordan, and a tomb inscribed with this name may be that of a person of that name active in Nehemiah's day.

By the fourth century Greek influences begin to appear. The first coins struck with a Hebrew inscription in Palestinian Aramaic characters name the province *Yhd* (Judah; see fig. 96). The same name appears on stamped jar handles found at scattered sites in the area. The art of the Persian period in Palestine is of a high order with finely worked silver bowls similar in design to the royal vessel of Darius II (fig. 72).

74, 75. *The oldest manuscript of a complete book of the Old Testament. The Scroll of Isaiah (IQ Is*ª*) found in Cave 1 at Qumran, near the Dead Sea, in 1947. It is open at column 33 showing Isaiah xl. 2-28. This column is shown enlarged on the left.*

Qumran. *c.* 100 BC. Leather. 10½ in. high. (Scroll 23 ft. 10 in. long). Jerusalem.

CHAPTER VI

IN NEW TESTAMENT TIMES

The discovery of the 'Dead Sea Scrolls' in 1947-56 has proved of great importance for the understanding of both Old and New Testaments. Since the first chance find of seven complete scrolls in a cave at Wadi Qumran, near the west coast of the Dead Sea, more than 200 similar places used for hiding manuscripts have been examined. In a collection of 400 texts, one hundred are biblical, representing all the books of the Hebrew canon except Esther. The best known is, perhaps, the complete scroll of Isaiah dated in the first century BC (figs. 74, 75), while other fragments or parts of scrolls on papyrus and leather range in date from c. 200 BC (Samuel, Jeremiah) to 68 AD for those found at Qumran, and to 132-135 AD for those found at the more southerly caves of Wadi Muraba'at excavated by De Vaux. The most copied books, according to the finds at Cave IV, were Deuteronomy (14 MSS), Isaiah (12) and the Psalms (10). It is interesting to note that these are the books most frequently quoted in the New Testament and in the teaching of Jesus Christ. This may be due to the fact that they would have been those best known by the common people through their use as educational works.

Until these discoveries were made, the oldest extant Hebrew MS had been the small Nash papyrus of part of Deuteronomy, dated by Albright

76. *Head of Augustus Caesar, Emperor of Rome (29 BC–14 AD) at the time of the birth and boyhood of Jesus Christ in Palestine (Luke ii. 1). He is shown in the prime of life. (See also fig. 89.)*

c. 29 BC–14 AD. Fine Greek marble. 1 ft. 9 in. high. BM Sculp. 1877.

77. *Bust of Tiberius as an old man wearing a veil. The treatment of the head and hair is as in portraits of the Claudian house. Tiberius was the Roman Emperor who ruled till a few years after the crucifixion (Luke iii. 1; John xix. 12, 15). His image appears on the 'penny' handed to Jesus Christ (Matthew xxii. 17-21; cf. fig. 90).*

Capri. 14-37 AD. Parian marble. 1 ft. 6½ in. high.   BM Sculp. 1881.

in the second or early first century BC. Now we have ample evidence for the three major textual traditions current in the days of Jesus Christ. Some of the MSS, such as the Isaiah scroll, have close affinity with the Massoretic text, which was stabilized by the first century AD, others with the long neglected Old Samaritan tradition, and others with the Alexandrian Septuagint. This latter is now shown, at least in the historical books, to be a faithful and literal reproduction of the Hebrew text as used in Egypt, and probably in Palestine, in the second century BC. Most of the fragments are still unpublished, but sufficient is known to show that these finds are of the greatest importance for the textual (lower) criticism of the Old Testament. Already their possible bearing on higher critical studies (questions of authorship and date) can be seen. Some late Hellenistic dates, to which part of Isaiah and Ecclesiastes have been ascribed, are now precluded.

The Dead Sea Scrolls also have an important bearing on New Testament studies. The non-biblical texts include commentaries and works showing the theology and organization of a Jewish sect, identified by most scholars as the Essenes. Archaeological work shows that the Qumran community flourished until it was dispersed by the Roman invasion in 68 AD when the documents were hidden.

Twelve miles from Qumran Jesus Christ was born at Bethlehem (c. 7 BC). Augustus Caesar was the Roman Emperor (fig. 76) and the rule of the Maccabees had been replaced by the family of Herod. A census under the local Roman governor Sulpicius Quirinius is known in 6-7 AD and these, according to other texts, occurred about every fourteen years. An Egyptian papyrus records a census in 104 AD for which everyone had to return to his ancestral home (cf. Luke ii. 1-3).

The ministry of Jesus took place while Tiberius was Emperor at Rome in 14-37 AD (fig. 77). His image was on the 'penny' handed to Christ (fig. 90). The kingdom of Herod the Great (37-4 BC) had been divided on his death among his three sons, each of whom adopted the name of Herod, a fact which sometimes confuses the reader of the Gospels. Archelaus, ethnarch of Judah (4 BC-6 AD; see fig. 86), was the Herod of Christ's boyhood; Herod Antipas, the tetrarch of Galilee and Upper Transjordan (4 BC-39 AD; see fig. 86), is the most frequently mentioned in the Gospels, while the tetrarch Herod Philip (4 BC-34 AD; see fig. 85) ruled N.E. Galilee. When Archelaus was exiled for misgovernment Judaea was administered by Roman procurators responsible in military affairs to the legate of Syria. Augustus respected the Jewish religion and customs, contributing to the Temple sacrifices. But he held his local representatives responsible for civil order, including the imposition of the death penalty. Coins of Pontius Pilate, procurator (26-36 AD) at the time of the death of Jesus Christ, have been found (see fig. 92).

An inscription, said to have come from Nazareth in 1878 (fig. 78), adds to the historical background of the resurrection. It is an 'ordinance of Caesar' demanding trial of anyone who 'has in any way extracted the buried or maliciously transferred them to another place . . . or has displaced the sealing or other stones'. There is, however, uncertainty as to the precise date of this text and whether it is an imperial decree or local rescript. If Augustan, the earliest date palaeographically possible according to Zulueta, it would show that the law demanding the death penalty on any who removed a body from a sealed tomb was in force at the time of the resurrection in Roman Palestine. The action attributed to the disciples by the priests would then have been construable as a serious crime. If, however, as Momigliano argues, the inscription is to be dated about 50 AD, it would have been part of the action taken by Claudius (fig. 80) to settle the disturbances among Jews in his Empire which he might well have attributed, in part, to the differences between their leaders and those who preached the resurrection of Jesus Christ of Nazareth. Claudius expelled the Jews from Rome (Acts xviii. 2) following riots 'at

78. *An ordinance demanding the death penalty on anyone who broke the seals on a tomb and moved or stole a dead body. It may have been set up in our Lord's birthplace in connection with allegations made against the disciples (Matthew xxviii. 11-15).*

Nazareth. *c.* 50 AD. White marble. 2 ft. high.
Louvre.

the instigation of one Chrestos' (Suetonius). A rescript of his in 41 AD concerning Alexandria appears to concern early Christian missionaries: 'If they do not abstain from their conduct I shall proceed against them for fermenting a malady common to the world.' Nero, his successor, continued his hostility to the Christian Church.

A number of Roman tombs of the first century have been discovered with a characteristic 'cartwheel' stone used to seal the entrance (fig. 79). Sukenik and other Jewish scholars have examined many tombs around Jerusalem. All date between the first century BC and the destruction of Jerusalem in 70 AD. Many ossuaries have been found, some of which, with their Aramaic and Greek inscriptions, Sukenik calls 'the earliest records of Christianity'. Names like Simon, Lazarus, Judas, Ananias and Jeshua (Jesus), one a son of Joseph, Miriam (Mary), Martha, Elisabeth, Salome, Johanna, Sapphira, do not mean that these represent the persons mentioned in the Bible for such names were common. A few names like Apphia (Philemon 2) and Barsabas (Acts i. 23, xv. 22) are uncommon outside the New Testament and it has been suggested that the tombs inscribed with these names may be theirs. On one epitaph Theodotion is called *didaskalos*, 'teacher' (in Hebrew, 'Rabbi'), a term once thought to have been anachronistic when used of Jesus Christ. One unusual inscription found by Sukenik in 1931 (fig. 100) shows the care with which the bones of notables were transferred when this became necessary. It may well be significant that in the first century AD the usual tomb equipment of pots and glass vessels to provide for the future needs of the deceased was gradually replaced by lamps (cf. fig. 116), often marked with the seven-branched Jewish *menorah*, the symbol of life and light. This may reflect a change in theological views on the after-life and on man's own inability to provide for it.

79. *A typical rock-hewn tomb of the first century* AD *with the circular stone used for sealing the grave when in use.*

One major source for the understanding of the religious outlook of the time is now the Dead Sea Scrolls. The non-biblical texts among them enable the views of the Essene sect to be described in detail. Similarities with John's Gospel, including, among other things, the ethical dualism of light and darkness, baptism and the celebration of holy communion, are leading to a reappraisal of this New Testament book which was once thought by some scholars to have been written under Hellenistic influences. Others find parallels in these texts with the teaching of the early Church regarding community of goods and with its distinctive methods and language used in biblical interpretation. The view has been advocated by Dupont-Sommer, and popularized by Edmund Wilson, that Christianity was in a measure based on the teaching of these Essenes. Allegro and a few others have asserted that the 'Teacher of Righteousness', a dominant but enigmatic figure in the Habakkuk commentary from Qumran, whose death, it is said, can be read in the text, anticipates Jesus Christ. These interpretations have been denied by most other scholars, among them Cross, Dupont-Sommer, Albright, Rowley and Young, and the commentary itself is probably to be dated before 41 BC. The remarkable differences between the aim and scope of the teaching of the Master in the scrolls and of Jesus Christ, the Messiah of the New Testament, must not be overlooked. This is especially true of such subjects as the salvation of the individual and the community. It is known, moreover, that there were a number of claimants to Messiahship (though it is not certain that the Qumran Teacher himself made such a claim), and that there were Jewish sects which based much of their teaching on the exposition of the Old Testament Scriptures in much the same way as did the early Christian Church. Until all these manuscript finds have been published and their meaning elucidated, dogmatism must be avoided when parallels are drawn.

The material background of the time of Jesus Christ can be viewed in

80. *Head of Claudius Caesar, the Roman Emperor twice mentioned in the book of the Acts (xi. 28, xviii. 2). He may have been the originator of the Nazareth decree (see fig. 78). Paul's appeal and subsequent imprisonment in Rome was in the reign of Nero (57-71 AD).*
41-54 AD. Marble. 8¼ in. high.
BM Sculp. 1951-3-30, I.

81. *Titus, son of Vespasian, Roman Emperor 69-79* AD, *whose armies besieged and sacked Jerusalem in 67-70* AD. *The capture of this city is commemorated on coins (fig. 93) and on the triumphal arch erected in 94* AD *in his honour at Rome. On this Jewish captives are shown carrying in procession the spoil from the Temple.*

Rome. *c.* 69-79 AD. Italian marble. 1 ft. 4½ in. high.   BM Sculp. 1841.

the buildings of Herod the Great, a great lover of Greek culture, who used income derived from heavy taxation for many constructional schemes. The retaining wall of the Temple was rebuilt down to bedrock and the area extended by a terrace supported by pillars, found in 1867-70 by Warren in the so-called 'Stables of Solomon'. Traces of Herodian masonry, including individual stones more than five metres long, are visible in the 'wailing wall', and in the first and part of the third walls circumscribing the old city. But of the unfinished Temple nothing remains after the total sack of the city by Titus (fig. 81) in 70 AD (Mark xiii. 2). Traces of early Jerusalem include the 2,500-metre square Roman Stone Pavement (the *Lithostroton* or *Gabbatha* of John xix. 13), identified by Vincent in the excavations beneath the later Hadrianic 'Ecce Homo' Arch. Marks of a game played by the Roman soldiers can still be seen cut in the stones.

Herod I, an Idumean by birth, also restored sites of historic national importance in order to ingratiate himself with the Jews. His work can be seen at the cave of Machpelah (Hebron) and at nearby Mamre (Abraham's Oak). He rebuilt Samaria, renamed Sebaste to honour Augustus, constructed a luxurious winter palace at Wadi Qelt near Jericho, Herodium his palace and burial place near Bethlehem, the city and port of Caesarea, and the towns of Phasaelis and Antipatris.

Significant finds in 1871 and 1935 were two of the large inscriptions (fig. 101) placed prominently at the Temple entrances at the time of Christ and the apostles, which read 'No stranger may enter within the balustrade round the Temple enclosure. Whoever is caught is alone responsible for his death which will follow.' This gives added meaning to the accusation brought by the Jews against Paul (Acts xxi. 28) and to his subsequent use of this as an illustration of the meaning and effect of the death of Jesus Christ (Ephesians ii. 13-19).

The journeys of Paul have been greatly elucidated from researches in

Asia Minor and Syria. A Latin inscription (Beirut Museum) records the work of 'Queen Bernice, daughter of King Agrippa (I), and King Agrippa (II) her brother' (figs. 87, 88) in restoring the buildings of Herod I at Caesarea. Antioch-on-the-Orontes of Paul's day is well known, and major sites such as the city of Ephesus, with its remains of the temple of Artemis, the Greek 'Diana of the Ephesians' (fig. 82), have been the subject of much attention by archaeologists. Statues of the multibreasted goddess, whose worship was combined with oriental fertility-beliefs, have recently been found there. Her massive temple, one of the seven wonders of the ancient world, was supported by a hundred columns, some of them sculptured (fig. 83).

At Ephesus the festival month of Artemision, when crowds of visitors flocked into the city (whose normal population then exceeded a quarter of a million), was no doubt viewed by Paul as an opportunity for preaching not to be missed (1 Corinthians xvi. 8-9). An inscription of 'Demetrius son of Menophilus' may refer to Paul's opponent there (Acts xix. 24). 'Asiarch' as applied to Ephesian officials is correctly applied by Luke according to contemporary inscriptions.

82. (*Left.*) *Silver didrachm showing the head of the Greek Artemis, the 'Diana of the Ephesians' of Acts xix. 28. The reverse shows a stag and a bee, symbols of the goddess.*
Ephesus. 258-202 BC. Silver. $\frac{13}{16}$ in. diameter.
Harvard University.

83. (*Right.*) *The sculptured drum of one of the eight columns supporting the pediment of the Artemision, or Temple of Diana, at Ephesus.*
c. 330 BC (destroyed 262 AD). Island marble.
5 ft. 11¾ in. high.　　BM Sculp. 1206.

84. *Bronze coin of Herod the Great (37-4 BC), king of Judaea at the time of Christ's birth (Matthew ii. 1-22; Luke i. 5). A headdress or incense altar between two palm branches.* 37-4 BC. BM Cat. Palestine. pl. xxiii. 14.

85. *Bronze coin of Herod Philip II (4 BC-34 AD), tetrarch of Auranitis and Batanea (Matthew xiv. 3-11; Mark vi. 17-28; Luke iii. 19). Head of Augustus, inscription, branch of laurel. Temple built by Herod to honour Augustus. Date between the columns.* 30 AD. BM Cat. Palestine. pl. xxiv. 31.

86. *Bronze coins. Left. Herod Antipas (4 BC-39 AD), tetrarch of Galilee and Peraea during Christ's ministry (Matthew xiv. 1-10, etc.). Dated 33/34 AD. Right. Herod Archelaus, ethnarch of Judaea, 4 BC (Matthew ii. 22) until banished in 6 AD. Wreath (as reverse of coin of Antipas).* BM Cat. Palestine. pl. xxv. 5 and 14.

87. *Bronze coin with head of Agrippa I (37-44 AD) with diadem. He is called by the family name of Herod in Acts xii. The reverse shows his son Agrippa II on horseback. Dated, beneath horse, year '2'.* 38/39 AD. G. F. Hill, *Thirty Pieces of Silver*, p. 237.

88. *Bronze coin of Agrippa II (50-100 AD) bearing a portrait of the Roman Emperor, Domitian, and on the reverse Tyche holding ears of barley and cornucopiae. Agrippa, before whom Paul was brought (Acts xxv. 13-xxvi. 32), minted coins in a Roman-Hellenistic style.* 95 AD. Reduced to two-thirds. BM Cat. Palestine. pl. xxvii. 13.

89. *Silver stater of Antioch, showing the head of Caesar Augustus. On the reverse Antioch, seated, and Orontes. The traitor Judas might have been paid with such 'pieces of silver' (Matthew xxvi. 15; cf. Luke xv. 8). See also fig. 95. 5 AD. BM Cat. Syria. pl. xx. 13.*

90. *Silver denarius of Tiberius current throughout the empire. Design: Head of Tiberius laureate. Reverse: Livia as Pax seated holding branch and sceptre. This common coin is the 'penny' brought to Jesus Christ (see Luke xx. 24). 14-37 AD. BM Cat. Roman Empire II. pl. xxii. 22.*

91. *The bronze asarion of Tyre. In use in the time of Tiberius whose head is shown, with laurel wreath and date. This coin is the 'farthing' mentioned by Jesus Christ (Matthew v. 26, x. 29). 32 AD. BM Cat. Syria. pl. xx.*

92. *Bronze coin of Pontius Pilate, procurator of Judaea at the time of the crucifixion (26-36 AD). Obverse: Three ears of corn, central upright, others drooping. Reverse: Vessel resembling simpulum. 29/30 AD. BM Cat. Palestine. pl. xxix. 3.*

93. *Bronze sestertius of Vespasian inscribed JUDAEA CAPTA. It commemorates the capture of Jerusalem and Judaea (67-70 AD). Centre, a palm-tree, the symbol of Judaea. A mourning Jewess sits on the right, with a captive Jew to the left. Head of Vespasian 71 AD. Reduced to two-thirds. BM Cat. Roman Empire II. pl. xx. 5.*

94. *View of the Parthenon from the north-west. This temple was built in 447-432 BC on the Acropolis, the fortress and religious centre of Athens. It was dedicated to the cult of the maiden goddess Athena, whose huge gold and ivory statue stood within. The pediment of the temple, supported on a porch with six Doric columns of Pentelic marble, could have been visible to Paul as he preached on the nearby Areopagus hill (Acts xvii. 22-31). Sculptures from the pediment and friezes ('Elgin Marbles') are in the British Museum.*

At Athens the market-place (*agora*), where Paul disputed daily, has been cleared and restored since 1930 by the American School of Classical Studies. The ruins of the Parthenon, the temple of Athena, which crowns the Acropolis (fig. 94), can be seen from the bare Areopagus, a hill 150 feet below to the north-west where the Athenian religious court met (Acts xvii. 19-31). An altar dedicated 'to the unknown god' has been found at Pergamum but not as yet at Athens.

At Corinth excavations since 1858 have uncovered shops similar to those where Paul must have worked (Acts xviii. 2-3). An inscription of 'Lucius the butcher' may indicate the presence of a meat-market (1 Corinthians x. 25). There is also a public square and rostrum where Paul was presented to the people by Gallio, whose rule as proconsul of Achaia in 51 AD is known from an inscription (Acts xviii. 12-17).

'Erastus' of Corinth occurs on another inscription (Romans xvi. 23). The 'proconsul Paulus' (Acts xiii. 7), the praetors of Philippi, the *protos* or Governor of Malta (xxviii. 7) and the 'politarchs' of Thessalonica (fig. 99) are but a few of the accurate observations of the historian Luke. Statues of Zeus and Hermes (Jupiter and Mercury) to whom Paul and Barnabas were likened have been found near Lystra. Derbe, a small site in the province of (South) Galatia, was identified by M. Ballance at Karti Hüyük, near Karaman, in 1956. From Laodicea, ten miles west of Colossae, the ruins of which were first explored in 1835, comes an inscription of Epaphras. The lukewarm water supply had to be brought by aqueduct when the local cooler springs failed (cf. Revelation iii. 15).

Among discoveries important for the study of the New Testament has been the finding of many thousands of papyri dated between the fourth century BC and the eighth century AD. These supplement the scarce, formal and monumental inscriptions with abundant detail. Many of them are written in the current *lingua franca* or *koinē* Greek. Finds made at Behnesa (Oxyrhynchus) in Egypt by Grenfell and Hunt in 1897 and

MISCELLANEOUS COINS

95. *Silver tetradrachm of Tyre and Antioch in current use in Palestine from 125 BC to 70 AD. Since it was current at the time of the crucifixion this may have been the 'piece of silver' used to bribe Judas (cf. fig. 89). The reverse shown is that of another coin, dated 27 AD. BM. G. F. Hill, op. cit., figs. 70-71.*

96. *The earliest Hebrew coin struck in Judah. Inscribed in Aramaic yhd (Yehud or Judah, once wrongly read as YHW). The design shows a male deity seated on a chariot holding a hawk, with square frame. First half 4th century BC. BM Cat. Palestine. pl. xix. 29.*

97. *Silver 'shekel of Israel, Year 1', often attributed to the time of Simon Maccabeus, but certainly of the First Revolt. Chalice with knob or star. Reverse: Stem with three flowers, inscribed 'Jerusalem the Holy (city)'. 66/67 AD. BM Cat. Palestine. pl. xxx. 1.*

98. *Silver tetradrachm, equivalent of a shekel, of Barcochba, leader of the Second Jewish Revolt (132-135 AD). Obverse shows a view of the Temple (or synagogue) with shrine containing scroll of the law. Inscribed 'Simeon'. Reverse: Palm-branch (lulab) and citrus ('ethrog). Inscribed 'Deliverance of Jerusalem'. BM Cat. Palestine. pl. xxxii. 8.*

99. *Greek inscription once incorporated in a Roman arch (the 'Gate of Vardar') at Thessalonica. Salonica was once one of the largest cities in Greece, being second only to Athens. In the time of Paul its city officials were designated 'politarchs'. The text names six such dignitaries, who are also mentioned in other inscriptions, including a dedication to Claudius in 44 AD when two were named. Luke correctly uses the term 'politarch' in Acts xvii. 6, 9, vindicating at this point, as in a number of other details, the accuracy of observation which marks his history.*

Thessalonica. 143 AD. White marble. 6 ft. 9½ in. long.   BM Inscrip. 171.

thereafter, the publication of the Chester Beatty and other collections of Greek papyri (including the extra-canonical *Logia Iesu* and Gospel of Thomas), have made many types of literature and script available for study. A typical letter is shown in fig. 103. The gain for the understanding of individual New Testament words and expressions is immeasurable. Among the manuscripts which have been found are an early Harmony of the Gospels and fragments of codices dating from the third century AD, more than a century older than the almost complete biblical text in the Codex Sinaiticus (fig. 104) and the Codex Vaticanus. A fragment of John (xviii. 21-33, 37-38), published by Roberts in 1935 and now in Manchester, is confidently dated to the first half of the second century AD. It is the oldest known fragment of the New Testament and shows the early spread of Christianity to Egypt. This Gospel, once commonly regarded as one of the latest books of the New Testament to have been written, is increasingly being shown to have been of an earlier date. Study of the non-biblical Dead Sea Scrolls and of the Gnostic (e.g. Bodmer) papyri recently found in Egypt, is leading to the view that all the Gospels may have been written before 70 AD and the whole of the New Testament perhaps as early as *c.* 85 AD. A codex of Paul's letters (Chester Beatty 11) shows these in collected form as early as 200 AD. The discoveries seem, at present, to imply also that the Christians predominantly used the codex (book) form for their writings as opposed to the non-Christian continued use of the roll. This may have been due to the need for ease of reading, reference and transportation. The textual discoveries confirm the view, well expressed by Sir Frederick Kenyon, that 'the interval between the dates of original composition and the earliest extant evidence becomes so small as to be in fact negligible, and the last foundation for any doubt that the Scriptures have come down to us substantially as they were written has now been removed. Both the *authenticity* and the *general integrity* of the books of the New Testament may be regarded as finally established'.

100. *This inscription, the longest Aramaic inscription from the time of Jesus Christ, was discovered by Sukenik in 1931. It states that 'hither were brought the bones of Uzziah, king of Judah—do not open!' The reburial may have been made necessary by the constructional work of Agrippa II in Jerusalem.*

Jerusalem. 1st century AD. Stone. 14 in. wide.

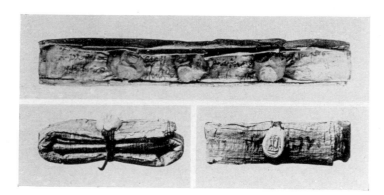

101. (*Left.*) *Inscription forbidding Gentiles to enter the inner court of the Temple on the pain of death. Standing in the time of Christ and the apostles.*

Jerusalem. *c.* 30 AD. White limestone, red letters. 2 ft. 10 in. wide. Istanbul Museum.

102. (*Above.*) *Papyrus rolled and sealed on the outside for despatch. It shows how Paul's letters might have been carried.*

Elephantine. 8th–4th centuries BC. Berlin.

103. *A typical letter written in a large semi-cursive hand. Procleius asks Pecusis to send him some drugs to Alexandria by the hand of his friend Sotas.*

1st century AD. 4 in. wide. BM Papyrus 356.

104. *A double folio of the Codex Sinaiticus (Luke xix. 30–xx. 34), one of the earliest and most important complete manuscripts of the whole Bible (the others being the Codices Alexandrinus and Vaticanus). Written in Greek 'biblical uncials' on a vellum codex.* Sinai. 4th century AD. Reduced to one-fifth. BM Add. MSS. 43725.

CHAPTER VII

METHODS AND RESULTS

The brief account of some archaeological discoveries given in the previous chapters presupposes some knowledge of the history of excavation in the ancient Near East and the development and use of scientific methods which enable comparisons to be made between archaeological and biblical studies.

The acquisition of the data needed to fill gaps in our knowledge of peoples, places or periods of history, is today the spur to most archaeological efforts in the Near East rather than, as formerly, the bearing of possible discoveries on the Bible. But a genuine interest in any results which relate to the Bible still remains. In the post-Renaissance centuries pilgrims and travellers made their way to holy sites like Jerusalem, the identity and location of which had never been forgotten, and noted the upstanding remains of temples and other large monuments in Palestine and its neighbouring countries. But only a few, like Pietro della Valle in 1650, recorded their impressions of the many 'ruin-mounds' (often locally named Tell, Khirbet or Hüyük) which are a characteristic of the ancient Near East (fig. 105). These artificial mounds were formed by the accumulation of rubbish of all sorts and by one generation building upon the levelled debris of its predecessor's dwellings. Towns were often abandoned

105, 106. (*Above.*) *The ruin-mound at Sultan Tepe, near Harran.* (*Below.*) *Erbil, a town built upon the ruins of centuries of previous occupation.*

95

107. *Air view showing the progress of the excavations at Ur in 1926. The ground-plan of the temples and adjacent buildings at the foot of the ziggurat (fig. 19) can be seen. The fan-shaped marks are the dumps of excavated earth thrown clear of the main site by use of a light railway.*

for reasons such as the failure of the water supply or devastation in time of war. In consequence the mud-brick structures were exposed to the levelling hand of rain and wind. When repeatedly occupied in this way for a number of successive periods some mounds became large and distinctive features of the countryside.

In 1839 the American Edward Robinson undertook valuable topographical researches in Palestine, accurately identifying many biblical sites from their situation and their arabic names. This method, however, was not without obvious dangers. The Palestine Exploration Fund, founded in 1865, produced the first modern map of the country based on its surveys, and commenced excavation at Jerusalem. Surface exploration, of special importance in Palestine because of frequent changes in political conditions, owes much to such men as Clermont-Ganneau and, more recently, to Nelson Glueck (for the Negeb and E. Jordan) and to Israeli scholars. The information gained has transformed our knowledge of biblical geography.

In Asia Minor the British interest in archaeology followed the rediscovery of the Hittites by A. H. Sayce in 1871, and this interest has been consistently furthered by the British Institute of Archaeology at Ankara. Excavations in Turkey by German and Turkish scholars have concentrated mainly at Boghazkoi, the Hittite capital, and at Kultepe and Kara-tepe in the south. Exploration of the New Testament sites antedates this and owes most to the careful industry of Sir William Ramsay, who has probably done more than any other single scholar to further the understanding of this area as it was in the first century AD.

Further east in Ancient Mesopotamia (modern Iraq) the reports of Rich and other travellers were followed up by the excavators, Botta working at Khorsabad in 1843, A. H. Layard and his assistant Rassam from 1845 at Nineveh, Calah (Nimrud) and in Babylonia. Layard was well before his time in carefully recording the circumstances in which he made his finds but, as in all early excavations, most attention was paid to acquiring large sculptures and monuments for the museums of Europe.

In Egypt the first scientific description of the country and its monuments was made by the savants who accompanied Napoleon's expedition in 1798. By 1822 Young and Champollion had deciphered the Egyptian hieroglyphic script on the basis of the Rosetta stone (fig. 32). Subsequently records of the standing antiquities were made by Lepsius, and by Mariette of the earliest excavations. These set a high standard for later Egyptological studies. A leading Egyptologist, Flinders Petrie, having evolved a system of sequence-dating by pottery, applied it when excavating at Tell el Hesi in S.W. Palestine in 1890. In the absence of inscriptions he sought to distinguish the various periods of occupation by the pottery found in each level and thus pioneered a scheme of Palestinian stratigraphy and typology which his successors developed, especially at Tell Beit Mirsim (1926-32), Samaria (1931-35), Lachish (1932-38) and Jericho (1952-58). In Iraq scientific exploration can be said to have begun with the German expedition to Babylon (1899-1914) and Assur (1902-14). The major sites of Syria (Byblos, Ras Shamra and Mari) have been excavated by French scholars with great care and outstanding results.

In modern times concessions for excavations are given by the government of the country concerned only to approved Institutions or research foundations. The expedition normally consists of archaeologist, surveyor, photographer, epigraphist, recorder and restorer. These supervise the local labourers who do the actual digging. On a large site where much overlay may have to be removed, as many as three hundred men and boys may be employed. Using picks, shovels and baskets the soil is carried clear of the digging by hand or by a light railway (fig. 107). The mound may have been first chosen because of its locality, or for the potential results which some chance discovery or surface finds forecast. Such finds often reveal the general date of occupation. The mound is first surveyed,

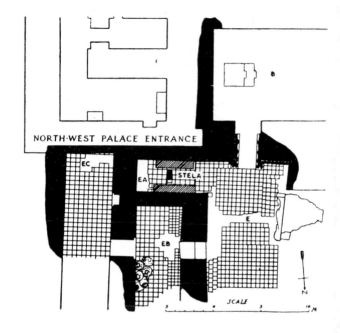

108. *Architect's plan of the palace entrance at Nimrud where the stele shown on fig. 43 was found. The excavations by The British School of Archaeology in Iraq in 1951 added to the plan (in outline) made by Layard a hundred years earlier. See e.g. fig. 46.*

photographed and subdivided into working areas. Ideally, the latest and uppermost level of occupation is then cleared and planned. Before the remains of this level are removed the exact location of every building and find is recorded, photographed and mapped (cf. fig. 108), and the process is then repeated at earlier, underlying levels. Since the occupation of any one period is rarely at one level, and buildings are often re-used, the interrelation of periods must be checked by stratigraphical cross sections. In practice, limited time and means may dictate that sounding trenches be cut at selected points to ascertain the general sequence of occupation or to locate a particular building.

In assessing the significance of the finds, inscriptions play an important part, often bringing a vividness to ordinary discoveries, as well as providing a sure means of dating them. Fortunately most of the major scripts found in Bible lands can now be read. The cuneiform script was deciphered in 1847 on the basis of Rawlinson's copy of the Behistun rock

109. (*Upper left.*) *The trilingual royal inscription of Darius cut in this rockface at Behistun, Persia, led to the decipherment of the cuneiform script.*

110. (*Lower left.*) *General view of excavations in progress at Nimrud in 1953 (cf. fig. 108).*

111. (*Right.*) *Large vessel from Lachish with stamped inscription on handle. Scale 1 : 12.*

inscriptions (fig. 109). Objects are rarely found inscribed, though a few bear some mark of ownership (fig. 111) or dedication, or may be marked with their weight or capacity. Sometimes, however, it is possible to relate objects found with those described in the Bible. Thus, for example, the 'pitcher' (*kadh*) commonly used for carrying water, and once employed by Gideon's men for shielding their torches, is the common, round-bottomed, hole-mouthed jar of the twelfth–tenth centuries (Judges vii. 16). The sacred 'pillars' or stones (*masseboth*) set up to mark a sacred place may well be similar to those found at Hazor in 1957 (fig. 112), though other scholars equate the 'pillar' with large obelisks found at the temple sites

112. (*Left.*) *The sacred place in a Canaanite shrine showing the small seated basalt figure of the god Ba'al (cf. fig. 113) and a row of stelae or 'pillars', averaging 1 ft. high, one engraved with hands raised towards the sun and moon.*

Hazor (Area C, 1955). 14th–13th century BC.

113. (*Right.*) *Bronze statuette of the weather god Ba'al, brandishing a thunderbolt.*

Tyre. *c.* 14th century BC. $4\frac{3}{8}$ in. high.

BM 25096.

114. *Part of an ivory panel. It shows two sphinxes, standing back-to-back and with their wings touching. One of them advances towards a sacred tree. These creatures are the 'cherubim' of the Old Testament (cf. Exodus xxv. 20, etc.).* Nimrud 8th century BC. 3¼ in. high.

BM 118163.

of Bethshan, Byblos and Petra. Ba'al, the weather god, is depicted on statuettes (fig. 113) and on stone carvings. Many small female figurines (perhaps the *teraphim* or household gods) used in fertility rites have been found and may represent the Phoenician goddess Astart, who was the same as the Assyrian Ishtar or later Greek Venus.

Temples have been discovered at Gerizim and Ai (Middle Bronze Age) and at Ras Shamra, Lachish and Hazor (Late Bronze Age). At the latter site a huge altar weighing five tons (cf. Judges vi. 25) was found, with a large incense altar, devoted to the sun-god, still bearing on its top the ash and burning left by the sacrifices. It is often difficult, however, to identify with any certainty the site of holy places, especially open 'high places'. Cult objects found include horned incense altars from Megiddo and Assyrian sites and a silver-plated standard from Hazor which depicts serpents similar to those on a stele from Kirjath-sephar. The excavations at Mari and other sites have increased our knowledge of ancient temples and their furniture and the use to which they were put. At Shiloh the ruins of a Byzantine church, conforming to the dimensions of the tabernacle which once lodged there, are of special interest, since the Solomonic and Herodian Temples did not survive the fall of Jerusalem to invaders in 587 BC and 70 AD. For similar reasons the earliest synagogue is known only for its description in an inscription of Theodotos (dated before 70 AD) found at Jerusalem in 1914. This was probably the same building as the 'synagogue of the freedmen' of Acts vi. 9. Other synagogue remains in Palestine are dated in the second century or after.

The earliest church yet excavated is a private room in a house at Dura on the Euphrates equipped as a chapel in the third century AD. Despite the number of places traditionally indicated, no burial place of any apostle has ever been found. The recent detailed excavations beneath St. Peter's in Rome show that Constantine built a church there in the fourth century AD. Below this the site appears to have been principally a burial ground for wealthy pagan Roman families. A few small burial places may have been used by Christians, but all scholars agree that it is impossible to identify any of the remains from the earliest level uncovered (*c.* 160 AD) with Peter's tomb. It is indeed unlikely that, in the fierce persecutions under Nero, the bodies of Peter, Paul or any of the leading Christians could have been recovered. The catacombs, a series of underground galleries outside Rome which, it is estimated, cover more than five hundred miles, are dated after 160 AD. Here the Christians worshipped secretly in times of persecution, and here many were buried in the niches, enshrouded in Jewish fashion. These catacombs are a primary source for the study of early Christian art. Among the many interesting designs which have been found is the symbol of a fish, doubtless chosen because the letters of the word IXΘΥΣ were the initial letters of the Greek words for 'Jesus Christ, Son of God, Saviour'.

Archaeology is a collaboration between many different sciences. Every form of knowledge may be called upon to help identify, repair or reconstruct the finds. Thus the pottery will have to be cleaned, recorded, repaired and, by an examination of the varying shapes, types of clay and techniques of manufacture, a ceramic index and chronology prepared. By typological comparisons the affinities and movements of peoples and their commercial connections may be discovered. Weapons, instruments and many classes of finds, from architectural features to bodies from graves, have to be examined in the same detail with the aid of the specialist staff of laboratories and museums. New techniques are constantly being introduced to overcome the problems which arise; for example, the Carbon 14 dating method, based on the measurement of the residual radioactivity of carbon remaining in old materials which once formed part of living organisms, has recently been developed. Some of these techniques and methods are still in an experimental stage and the results are used, not as

115. *One of a number of letters from city-governors in Palestine appealing to the Egyptian king for help against rebels and incoming, semi-nomadic Habiru. The governor of Gubbu reports that all is now well. He, with his men and chariots, is ready to join the king's army wherever required.*

Tell el-Amarna. *c.* 1400 BC. 2½ in. high.

BM 29861.

the basis for dogmatic statements, but as providing a reasonable hypothesis on which to build the final picture which it is the aim of any expedition to provide.

Many problems, necessarily ignored in this brief survey, await further study and elucidation. If the points of direct contact between archaeology and the Bible, as distinct from general illustration, seem few, let it be remembered that scientific archaeological research in Bible lands is a comparatively recent development. Many promising sites are still unsearched and much remains to be studied and published. If progress is to be maintained in biblical archaeology as a scientific study great care is needed, both in the selection of facts from archaeology as a whole, and in the integration of the evidence with the proved results of Old Testament scholarship. For lack of this, much well-intentioned effort to 'prove the truth of the Bible' is rightly criticized.

The late Sir Frederick Kenyon, former Director of the British Museum, aptly summed up his survey of *Archaeology and the Bible* (p. 30) by stating his belief that 'the progress of archaeological research will be found to constitute a steady march in the direction of establishing the essential trustworthiness of the Bible narrative, and of greatly increasing our intelligent comprehension of it, and thereby our appreciation of its spiritual message, which constitutes its real value for mankind'.

Wise students will use the evidence of biblical archaeology to this end, so that God's Word to man may be 'a lamp to our feet and a light to our paths'.

116. *The most common lamp in use throughout Bible times was the simple, single wick 'slipper' type, with opening for replenishing the oil. In later New Testament times the spout was sometimes decorated with symbols.* 4½ in. long.

117. *This lamp with its open bowl is unusual in having seven places for the wick. It shows a rare development from the earlier, and common, open–dish type.*
Palestine. 2nd century AD. Bronze. 10½ in. long. BM 113191.

BIBLIOGRAPHY

One of the objects of this book is to encourage the reader to turn to more detailed and authoritative works on biblical archaeology. This bibliography aims to provide a list of some general works in English which cover the whole subject and also selected references by which it should be possible both to follow up the detail of the text and to obtain further illustrations of the matters discussed. Those books cited will guide to a full bibliography of works in all languages. The student who wishes to keep up to date with archaeological discoveries will do well to consult current numbers of journals.

GENERAL

Abbreviations used in later sections of the bibliography are shown in brackets following the title.

I. JOURNALS

Anatolian Studies (AS). The Journal of the British Institute of Archaeology at Ankara, 56 Queen Anne Street, London, W.I. (Principally covers Asia Minor).

The Biblical Archaeologist (BA). A Journal of the American Schools of Oriental Research, New Haven, U.S.A. (All subjects). British Agent: Blackwell, Broad Street, Oxford.

Bulletin of the American Schools of Oriental Research (BASOR). Address as above. (All ancient Near East).

Journal of Egyptian Archaeology (JEA). Journal of Egypt Exploration Society, 2 Hinde Street, London, W.I. (Egypt).

Journal of Near Eastern Studies (JNES). The Oriental Institute, Chicago. (All Near East).

Israel Exploration Journal (IEJ). The Hebrew University, Jerusalem. (Israel).

Iraq. Journal of British School of Archaeology in Iraq, 5 New Square, Lincoln's Inn, London, W.C.2. (Mainly Iraq, also Syria, Jordan, Persia).

Palestine Exploration Fund Quarterly (PEQ). Journal of Exploration Fund and British School of Archaeology in Jerusalem, 2 Hinde Street, London, W.I. (Jordan and Israel and related subjects).

Syria. Journal of l'Institut Français d'Archéologie de Beyrout. Published by Geuthner, Paris. (Mainly Syria).

Matters of biblical archaeology are also commented on by journals devoted to Old and New Testament Studies and fuller bibliographies are given in a number of journals, e.g. *The Annual Book List of the Society for Old Testament Studies (SOTS)*.

II. GENERAL WORKS

Old and New Testament discoveries with bibliographical notes.

W. F. ALBRIGHT. *Recent Discoveries in Bible Lands (RDBL)*, Pittsburg, 1955. *The Biblical Period (BP)*, New York, 1949; Oxford, 1952 (Reprint from *The Jews: their History, Culture and Religion*). *The Archaeology of Palestine (AP)*, London, 1954. *Archaeology and the Religion of Israel (ARI)*, Baltimore, 1953. *From the Stone Age to Christianity (SAC)*, Baltimore, 1940.

G. E. WRIGHT. *Biblical Archaeology (B.Arch)*, Philadelphia; London, 1957.

MILLAR BURROWS. *What Mean These Stones?* (*WMTS*), New Haven, 1941.

J. FINEGAN. *Light from the Ancient Past* (*LAP*), Princeton, 1946.

J. P. FREE. *Archaeology and Bible History*, Wheaton, 1950.

C. H. GORDON. *Introduction to Old Testament Times*, Ventnor, U.S.A., 1953.

III. GEOGRAPHY

L. H. GROLLENBERG. *Atlas of the Bible*, London, 1956.

G. E. WRIGHT and F. V. FILSON. *The Westminster Historical Atlas*, Philadelphia; London, 1947.

J. F. STIRLING. *Philip's Atlas of the New Testament*, London, 1951.

F. VAN DER MEER and C. MOHRMANN. *Atlas of the Early Christian World*, London, 1958.

G. ADAM SMITH. *The Historical Geography of the Holy Land*, London, 1931.

IV. TEXTS (IN TRANSLATION)

J. B. PRITCHARD (editor). *Ancient Near Eastern Texts relating to the Old Testament* (*ANET*), Princeton, 1955.

D. WINTON THOMAS (editor). *Documents from Old Testament Times* (*DOTT*), New York and London, 1958. (Smaller selection than *ANET* but with commentary).

V. VARIOUS

E. W. HEATON. *Everyday Life in Old Testament Times*, New York and London, 1956.

A. C. BOUQUET. *Everyday Life in New Testament Times*, New York and London, 1953.

A. BARROIS. *Manuel d'archéologie biblique*, I-II, Paris, 1939-53.

W. M. THOMSON. *The Land and the Book*, London, 1861 (and later editions).

CHAPTER I. THE DAWN OF CIVILIZATION

GENERAL

RDBL, pp. 60-72. *AP*, pp. 49-79. *SAC*, pp. 88-130. *B.Arch*, pp. 29-35.

H. H. FRANKFORT. *The Birth of Civilization in the Near East*, London, 1951.

A. T. CLAY. *The Origin of Biblical Traditions*, New Haven, 1932.

S. N. KRAMER. *From the Tablets of Sumer* (*FTS*), Colorado, 1956. (An English edition is entitled *History Begins with Sumer*, London, 1958). *Sumerian Mythology*, Philadelphia, 1944. *Biblical Parallels from Sumerian Literature*, Philadelphia, 1954.

TEXTS

Creation

ANET, pp. 60-72. *DOTT*, pp. 3-16. *FTS*, pp. 71-96 (for fig. 4).

A. HEIDEL. *The Babylonian Genesis*, Chicago, 1951.

P. J. WISEMAN. *Creation Revealed in Six Days*, London, 1948.

Pre-Flood

S. H. LANGDON. *Oxford Edition of Cuneiform Texts*, Vol. I, 1923 (for fig. 5).

Paradise

FTS, pp. 169-175, 259-262. *ANET*, pp. 37-42.

S. N. KRAMER. *Enmerkar and the Lord of Aratta*, Philadelphia, 1952.

Flood

FTS, pp. 176-181. *ANET*, pp. 93-97. *DOTT*, pp. 17-26.

A. HEIDEL. *The Gilgamesh Epic and Old Testament Parallels*, Chicago, 1949 (for fig. 10).

THE ANTIQUITY OF WRITING

S. H. LANGDON. *Excavations at Kish*, Vol. I, Paris, 1924, pp. 99-101 (for fig. 7). *Oxford Edition of Cuneiform Texts*, Vol. VII, 1926, pl. xxvi (wrongly numbered BM 116630; cf. fig. 8).

G. R. Driver. *Semitic Writing*, 1954, London, pp. 3-8.
A. Falkenstein. *Die archaische Texte aus Uruk*, Berlin, 1936.
S. N. Kramer. *FTS*, pp. xix-xxii, 227-280.

VARIOUS

A. Parrot. *The Flood and Noah's Ark*, London, 1955. *The Tower of Babel*, London, 1956.
C. L. Woolley. *Excavations at Ur*, London, 1954. *The Early Periods* (*Ur Excavations*, Vol. IV), London, 1956 (for fig. 11). *The Royal Cemetery* (*Ur Excavations*, Vol. II), London, 1934 (for figs. 12-17). *The Ziggurat and its Surroundings* (*Ur Excavations*, Vol. V), London, 1939 (for figs. 18, 19).
C. J. Gadd. *The History and Monuments of Ur*, London, 1929.
Sidney Smith. *Early History of Assyria*, London, 1931, p. 86 (for fig. 9).

CHAPTER II. THE PATRIARCHAL AGE

GENERAL

RDBL, pp. 72-78. *BP*, pp. 3-6. *AP*, pp. 80-109. *SAC*, pp. 150-207. *B.Arch*, pp. 40-52.

SPECIAL ASPECTS

C. H. Gordon. 'Biblical Customs in the Nuzu Tablets' in *BA*, III, 1944.
J. P. Harland. 'Sodom and Gomorrah' in *BA*, V, 1942; VI, 1943.

LAW CODES OF THE SECOND MILLENNIUM BC

ANET, pp. 159-180. *DOTT*, pp. 27-37.
G. E. Mendenhall. 'Ancient Oriental and Biblical Law' in *BA*, XVII, 1954, pp. 26-46. 'Abraham's Purchase of the Cave of Machpelah and Hittite Law' in *BASOR*, 129, 1953, pp. 15-18.

'CANAANITE' LITERATURE

ANET, pp. 129-155. *DOTT*, pp. 118-133.
G. R. Driver. *Canaanite Myths and Legends*, Edinburgh, 1956.
J. G. Gray. *The Legacy of Canaan, The Ras Shamra Texts and their Relevance to the Old Testament*, Leiden, 1957.
C. H. Gordon. *Ugaritic Handbook*, Rome, 1947.
C. Virolleaud. *La Légende phénicienne de Danel*, Paris, 1936 (for fig. 26). *Le Palais Royal d'Ugarit* (textes en cunéiforme alphabétiques), II, Paris, 1957.

OTHER TEXTS OF THE PERIOD

G. Dossin etc. *Archives royales de Mari*, I-IX, XV, Paris, 1950-58.
J. Nougayrol. *Le Palais royal d'Ugarit*, III-IV, Paris, 1955-56.
D. J. Wiseman. *The Alalakh Tablets*, London, 1953.

VARIOUS

M. Dothan. 'Some Aspects of Religious Life in Palestine during the Hyksos Rule' in *Antiquity and Survival*, II, Hague and Jerusalem, 1957, pp. 121-130.
P. J. Wiseman. *New Discoveries in Babylonia about Genesis*, London, 1948.

CHAPTER III. EGYPT AND THE EXODUS

GENERAL

RDBL, pp. 5-21, 77-78, 83-89. *BP*, pp. 6-17. *AP*, pp. 80-109. *BA*, pp. 53-84.
E. A. W. Budge and H. R. Hall. *Introductory Guide to the Egyptian*

Collections in the British Museum, London, 1930 (for figs. 29, 33, 34).

EGYPT

History

J. H. BREASTED. *A History of Egypt from the Earliest Times to the Persian Conquest*, London, 1925.
E. DRIOTON and J. VANDIER. *L'Egypte*, Paris, 1957.
W. C. HAYES. *The Scepter of Egypt*, New York, 1953.
G. STEINDORFF and K. SEELE. *When Egypt Ruled the East*, Chicago, 1957.

Texts

ANET, pp. 3-36, 227-263, 325-330. *DOTT*, pp. 137-191.
E. A. W. BUDGE. *The Rosetta Stone*, London, 1957 (for fig. 32). *The Book of the Dead Papyrus of Ani*, London, 1913 (for fig. 30).
W. C. HAYES. *A Papyrus of the Late Middle Kingdom in the Brooklyn Museum*, Yale University, 1955 (for fig. 31).
J. CERNY. *Paper and Books in Ancient Egypt*, London, 1947.

Funerary Rites and Furniture

N. DE G. DAVIES and A. H. GARDINER. *Ancient Egyptian Paintings*, Chicago, 1936.
N. DE G. DAVIES. *The Tomb of Rekhmire at Thebes*, New York, 1943 (for fig. 38).
A. MEKHITARIAN. *Egyptian Painting*, Geneva, 1954.
H. E. WINLOCK. *Models of Daily Life in Ancient Egypt*, New York, 1955.
J. H. BREASTED. *Egyptian Servant Statues*, Washington, 1948 (for fig. 28).
A. SHORTER and I. E. S. EDWARDS. *A Handbook to the Egyptian Mummies and Coffins exhibited in the British Museum*, London, 1938 (for fig. 39).

W. C. HAYES. *Royal Sarcophagi of the XVIIIth Dynasty*, Princeton, 1935.
E. A. W. BUDGE. *The Mummy*, Cambridge, 1925.
G. E. SMITH and W. DAWSON. *Egyptian Mummies*, London, 1924.

Architecture

I. E. S. EDWARDS. *The Pyramids*, London, 1947.
W. S. SMITH. *The Art and Architecture of Ancient Egypt*, London, 1958.

Techniques

A. LUCAS. *Ancient Egyptian Materials*, London, 1948.
C. F. NIMS. 'Bricks without Straw' in *BA*, XIII, 1950, pp. 22-28.

Various

P. MONTET. *Everyday Life in Egypt*, London, 1958.
J. CERNY. *Ancient Egyptian Religion*, London, 1952.
A. H. GARDINER. *Egyptian Grammar*, Oxford, 1957. 'The Delta Residence of the Ramessides' in *JEA*, 5, 1918, pp. 128 ff., 179 ff. 'The Geography of the Exodus' in *JEA*, 10, 1924, pp. 87-96.
A. LUCAS. *The Route of the Exodus*, London, 1938.
F. S. BODENHEIMER. 'The Manna of Sinai' in *BA*, XI, 1947, pp. 2-6.
F. M. CROSS. 'The Tabernacle' in *BA*, X, 1947, pp. 45-68.

THE CONQUEST OF CANAAN

H. H. ROWLEY. *From Joseph to Joshua*, London, 1950.
A. D. TUSHINGHAM. 'Excavations at Old Testament Jericho' in *BA*, XVI, 1953, pp. 46-67; XVII, 1954, pp. 98-104.
Y. AHARONI. 'Problems of the Israelite Conquest in the light of Archaeological Discoveries' in *Antiquity and Survival*, II, Hague and Jerusalem, 1957, pp. 131-150.

Also see various articles by W. F. ALBRIGHT in *BASOR*, 1935-58, and the publications on Palestinian sites quoted in the bibliography to the next chapter.

THE DEVELOPMENT OF THE ALPHABET

W. F. ALBRIGHT. 'The Earliest Alphabetic Inscriptions from Sinai and their Decipherment' in *BASOR*, 110, 194, pp. 6-22 (for fig. 41).
G. R. DRIVER. *Semitic Writing*, London, 1954, pp. 128-197 (cf. fig. 42).

CHAPTER IV. IN THE DAYS OF THE KINGS

GENERAL

RDBL, pp. 89-97. *BP*, pp. 23-24. *AP*, pp. 110-142. *B.Arch*, pp. 85-172.
A. PARROT. *Nineveh and the Old Testament*, London, 1957.

TEXTS

ANET, pp. 269-301 (Assyrian); pp. 320-321 (Palestinian). *DOTT*, pp. 46-75; 195-198 (Moabite Stone).
C. J. GADD. 'Inscribed Prisms of Sargon II from Nimrud' in *Iraq*, XVI, 1954, pp. 173-201.
N. AVIGAD. 'The Epitaph of a Royal Steward from Siloam Village' in *IEJ*, 3, 1953, pp. 137-152 (for fig. 53).
D. J. WISEMAN. 'A New Stela of Assur-nasir-pal II' in *Iraq*, XIV, 1952, pp. 24-44 (for fig. 43). 'A Fragmentary Inscription of Tiglath-pileser III from Nimrud' in *Iraq*, XVIII, 1956, pp. 117-124.

EXCAVATION REPORTS

O. TUFFNEL. *Lachish III*, London, 1953 (for figs. 65, 111).
G. A. REISSNER and C. S. FISHER. *Harvard Excavations at Samaria*, Cambridge, U.S.A., 1924.
J. W. CROWFOOT etc. *The Buildings at Samaria*, London, 1942. *Early Ivories from Samaria*, London, 1938.
R. S. LAMON and G. M. SHIPTON. *Megiddo I*, Chicago, 1939.
C. C. McCOWN. *Tell en-Nasbeh I-II*, New Haven, 1947.

W. F. ALBRIGHT. *The Excavation of Tell Beit Mirsim III*, New Haven, 1943.
Y. YADIN. *Hazor I*, Oxford and Jerusalem, 1958.
Other sites, including Dothan, Shechem, have been reported recently in *BASOR*.

VARIOUS

R. D. BARNETT. 'The Siege of Lachish' in *IEJ*, 8, 1958, pp. 161-164.
T. DOTHAN. 'Archaeological Reflections on the Philistine Problem' in *Antiquity and Survival*, II, 1957, pp. 151-164.
P. L. GARBER. 'Reconstructing Solomon's Temple' in *BA*, XIV, 1951, pp. 2-24.
N. GLUECK. *The Other Side of Jordan*, New Haven, 1940. *BASOR*, 90, 1943, pp. 2-23 (Israelite towns). *BASOR*, 91, 1943, pp. 7-26 (Moab).
G. E. MENDENHALL. *Law and Covenant in Israel and the Ancient Near East*, Pittsburgh, 1955.
A. PARROT. *Samaria, the Capital of the Kingdom of Israel*, London, 1958.
A. REIFFENBERG. *Ancient Hebrew Seals*, London, 1950.
J. SIMONS. *Jerusalem in the Old Testament*, Leiden, 1952, pp. 178-192 (Siloam tunnel; cf. fig. 55).
D. J. WISEMAN. 'Assyrian Writing Boards' in *Iraq*, XVII, 1955, pp. 3-13. *The Vassal-Treaties of Esarhaddon*, London, 1958 (for fig. 61).
G. E. WRIGHT. 'The Discoveries at Megiddo, 1935-1939' in *BA*, XIII, 1950, pp. 28-46.

CHAPTER V. THE EXILE AND AFTER

GENERAL

RDBL, pp. 98-106. *BP*, pp. 45-55. *AP*, pp. 142-145. *SAC*, pp. 256-292. *B.Arch*, pp. 172-179, 199-210.
J. FINEGAN. *Light from the Ancient Past*, Princeton, 1946, pp. 192 ff.

TEXTS

ANET, pp. 301-317 (for text of fig. 70), pp. 321-322 (Lachish Ostraca); pp. 491-492 (Elephantine papyri). *DOTT*, pp. 201-211 (for text of fig. 64); pp. 75-83 (for text, etc., of fig. 63); pp. 84-86 (for text of fig. 69).

D. J. WISEMAN. *Chronicles of Chaldaean Kings (626-556 BC) in the British Museum*, London, 1956 (for fig. 63).

F. F. WEIDNER. *Mélanges syriens offert à M. René Dussaud*, II, Paris, 1939, pp. 923-935 (for fig. 69).

E. G. KRAELING. 'New Light on the Elephantine Colony' in *BA*, XV, 1952, pp. 50-67.

G. R. DRIVER. *Aramaic Documents of the Fifth Century BC*, Oxford, 1954.

VARIOUS

A. PARROT. *Babylon and the Old Testament*, London, 1958.

R. KOLDEWEY. *The Excavations at Babylon*, London, 1914.

E. UNGER. *Babylon: die heilige Stadt nach der Beschreibung der Babylonier*, Berlin.

C. J. GADD. 'The Harran Inscriptions of Nabonidus' in *AS*, VIII, 1958, pp. 35-92.

CHAPTER VI. IN NEW TESTAMENT TIMES

GENERAL

J. FINEGAN. *Light from the Ancient Past*, Princeton, 1946.

G. H. DEISSMANN. *Light from the Ancient East*, New York and London, 1927.

RDBL, pp. 109-131. *AP*, pp. 146-176, 238-249. *B.Arch*, pp. 218-274.

A. C. BOUQUET. *Everyday Life in New Testament Times*, New York and London, 1953.

J. CARCOPINO. *Daily Life in Ancient Rome*, New Haven, 1940.

S. PEROWNE. *The Life and Times of Herod the Great*, London, 1956. *The Later Herods*, London, 1958.

TEXTS

F. G. KENYON. *Our Bible and the Ancient Manuscripts*, Oxford, 1957.

F. G. KENYON and I. BELL. *Greek Papyri in the British Museum*, III, London, 1907 (for census text).

T. C. SKEAT. *The Codex Sinaiticus and The Codex Alexandrinus*, London, 1955.

B. M. METZGER. 'Recently Published Greek Papyri of the New Testament' in *BA*, X, 1947, pp. 26-44.

F. F. BRUCE. *The Books and the Parchments*, London, 1950. *Are the New Testament Documents Reliable?*, London, 1953.

DEAD SEA SCROLLS

F. M. CROSS. *The Ancient Library of Qumran*, London, 1958.

MILLAR BURROWS. *The Dead Sea Scrolls*, New York, 1955. *More Light on the Dead Sea Scrolls*, London, 1958. *The Dead Sea Scrolls of St. Mark's Monastery*, I. Isaiah, New Haven, 1953 (for fig. 75).

F. F. BRUCE. *Second Thoughts on the Dead Sea Scrolls*, London, 1956.

J. VAN DER PLOEG. *The Excavations at Qumran*, London, 1958.

H. H. ROWLEY. *The Zadokite Fragments and the Dead Sea Scrolls*, Oxford, 1952 (for full bibliography of more than 500 works on this subject).

For a later bibliography consult the Book Lists of the *SOTS* and for the latest details *BA*, *BASOR*, *Revue Biblique* and *Vetus Testamentum*.

ST. PAUL'S JOURNEYS

H. METZGER. *St. Paul's Journeys in the Greek Orient*, London, 1956.

W. M. RAMSAY. *The Cities of St. Paul*, New York and London, 1908. *St. Paul the Traveller and Roman Citizen*, New York and London, 1896.

W. A. McDONALD. 'Archaeology and St. Paul's Journeys in Greek

Lands'—I in *BA*, III, 1940, pp. 18-24; II (Athens) in *BA*, IV, 1941, pp. 1-10.

SITES

C. WATZINGER. *Denkmäler Palästinas II*, Leipzig, 1935.

M. M. PARVIS and F. V. FILSON. 'Ephesus' in *BA*, VIII, 1945.

J. T. WOOD. *Discoveries at Ephesus*, London, 1877.

B. ASHMOLE. *Sculptures of the Parthenon*, London, 1952.

B. M. METZGER. 'Antioches-on-the-Orontes' in *BA*, XI, 1948.

S. E. JOHNSON. 'Laodicea and its Neighbours' in *BA*, XIII, 1950.

J. L. KELSO. 'New Testament Jericho' in *BA*, XIV, 1951, pp. 34-43.

L. MOWRY. 'Settlements in the Jericho Valley during the Roman Period (63 BC-AD 134)' in *BA*, XV, 1952, pp. 26-42.

R. O'CALLAGHAN. 'Vatican Excavations and the Tomb of St. Peter' in *BA*, XVI, 1953, pp. 70-87.

COINS

A. REIFFENBERG. *Ancient Jewish Coins*, Jerusalem, 1940. *Ancient Hebrew Arts*, New York, 1950 (also inscriptions). *Israel's History in Coins from the Maccabees to the Roman Conquest*, London, 1953.

G. F. HILL. *British Museum Catalogue of the Greek Coins of Palestine*, London, 1914.

A. KINDLER. 'Coins as Documents for Israel's Ancient History' in *Antiquity and Survival*, II, Hague and Jerusalem, 1957, pp. 225-236.

VARIOUS

W. M. RAMSAY. *The Bearing of Recent Discoveries on the Trustworthiness of the New Testament*, London, 1915.

C. M. COBERN. *The New Archaeological Discoveries and the Bearing upon the New Testament*, New York and London, 1917.

E. M. BLAIKLOCK. *Out of the Earth* (The witness of archaeology to the New Testament), London, 1957 (for fig. 78).

H. G. MAY. 'Synagogues in Palestine' in *BA*, VII, 1944.

For the Dead Sea Scrolls and the New Testament, see works cited in Bibliography to Chapter VI, especially F. F. BRUCE, *op. cit.* 'The Scrolls and Christianity', pp. 123-137.

CHAPTER VII. METHODS AND RESULTS

See also General Bibliography above.

EXCAVATION (TECHNIQUE)

N. GLUECK. 'What is Biblical Archaeology?' in *The Other Side of Jordan*, New Haven, 1940, pp. 1-32.

K. KENYON. *Beginning in Archaeology*, London, 1952. *Digging up Jericho*, London, 1957.

A. PARROT. *Discovering Buried Worlds*, London, 1955.

C. L. WOOLLEY. *Digging up the Past*, London, 1954.

E. CHIERA. *They Wrote on Clay*, Chicago, 1951.

VARIOUS

SETON LLOYD. *Foundations in the Dust*, London, 1955.

M. E. L. MALLOWAN. *Twenty-five years of Mesopotamian Archaeology*, London, 1956.

A. PALLIS. *The Antiquity of Iraq*, London, 1956.

R. B. K. AMIRAN. 'The Story of Pottery in Palestine' in *Antiquity and Survival*, II, Hague and Jerusalem, 1957, pp. 187-217.

J. GARROW DUNCAN. *Corpus of Palestinian Pottery*, London, 1930 (needs bringing up to date by reference to later Excavation reports as, e.g., those listed in Bibliography above). Cf. *AP*, pp. 48, 116, 131.

G. E. WRIGHT. 'Israelite Daily Life' in *Biblical Archaeology*, London, 1957, pp. 180-198.

H. J. PLENDERLEITH. *The Preservation of Antiquities and Works of Art*, Oxford, 1956.

GENERAL INDEX

Abiyau, seals of, 58
Abram, Abraham, 23, 25, 27 ff.
Achaia, 88
Adad-nirari III, 56, 58
Adam, 9
After-life, 34, 37, 82
Agrippa I, 85 f.
Agrippa II, 85 f., 91
Ahab, 55 f.
Ahaz, 66
Ai, 48, 100
Akhenaten, 41
Alalah, 25, 30, 39, 54
Alexandria, 82
Alphabetic script, 30, 48 f.
Altar, 20, 88, 100
Amarna, 37, 41, 101
Amarna Age, 25
Amenophis III, 40 f.
Ammon, 30
Amorites, 23
Amraphel, 30
Amun, 39, 41, 47, 55, 64
Ananias, 82
Antipas (Herod), 81, 84, 86
Apphia, 82
Aqueducts, 64, 88
Aramaeans, 27, 53, 58
Aramaic, 66, 70, 75, 82, 89, 91
Archelaus (Herod), 81, 86
Areopagus, 88
Arsham, 76
Artemis, 85

Artemision, 85
Asherah, 41
Ashkelon, 29, 48, 70
Ashur, 66
Ashurbanipal, 13, 66
Ashurnasirpal II, 50 f.
Asiarch, 85
Assur, 97
Assyria, 5 ff., 12 f., 25, 56 ff.
Astart, 41, 100
Athena, 88
Athens, 88
Augustus Caesar, 79 f., 84, 87
Avaris, 34, 41
Azariah, 58, 65
Azekah, 73

Ba'al, 30, 41, 58, 99 f.
Babel, Tower of, 20
Babylon, Babylonia, 9, 12, 20, 25, 27, 30, 60, 69 ff., 75 f., 97
Babylonian Chronicle, 69, 75
Bagoi, 76
Barsabas, 82
Behistun, 98
Belshazzar, 75
Benhadad, 56, 58
Benjamin, 23
Bethel, 29, 55, 73, 75
Bethlehem, 80, 84
Bethshan, 41, 46, 100
Bethshemesh, 53 ff., 73
Beth-zur, 53, 75
Boghazkoi, 30, 96

Book of the Dead, 37
Borsippa, 20
Brak, 25
Brickmakers, 42 ff.
Bricks, 43, 71
Byblos, 7, 97, 100

Caesarea, 84 f.
Calah, 51, 96
Calf, golden, 39
Canaan, entry into, 46, 48
Canaanite religion, 30
Canaanite temples, 54
Carbon 14 dating, 101
Carchemish, 69
Catacombs, 101
Census, 80
Chagar Bazar, 25
Cherubim, 54, 100
Chronology, 15, 25, 70, 101
Claudius, 81, 83, 90
Code of Laws, 27
Codex, 91
Codex Sinaiticus, 91, 94
Coins, 76, 86 f., 89
Colossae, 88
Corinth, 88
Covenant, 66
Creation, 7 f.
Cuneiform script, 10, 24 f., 41, 48, 64, 75, 98
Cylinder-seals, 9, 58, 75
Cyrus, 74 f.

Damascus, 56, 59
Darius the Mede, 75
Darius I, 75 ff., 98
Darius II, 76
David, 53
Dead Sea, 30, 54
Dead Sea Scrolls, 10, 78 ff., 83, 91
Debir, 46, 53, 55, 60, 73
Decipherment, 39, 98 f.
Demetrius, 85
Derbe, 88
Deuteronomy, 79
Diana of the Ephesians, 85
Dilmun, 9
Dothan, 29
Dura, 100

Ea, 7, 13
Ecclesiastes, 80
Edom, 46, 53, 55
Egypt, 3, 10, 28 f., 33 ff., 37
Egyptian decipherment, 39
Egyptian inscriptions, 37, 47
Egyptian religion, 44
Egyptian writing, 10, 47 ff.
Elath, 58
Elephantine, 76
Eliakim, 73
Elisabeth, 82
Embalming, 46 f.
Ephesus, 85
Erastus, 88
Erech, 13
Esarhaddon, 64, 66

Essenes, 80, 83
Euphrates, 12, 25, 41, 100
Eve, 9 f.
Excavation methods, 97 f.
Execration texts, 28
Exodus, 40 f., 43
Ezion-geber, 53, 58

Fall, 9 f.
Famine, 34
Figurines, 100
Flood, 8 f., 13 ff.
Flood-deposit, 14 f.

Gabbatha, 84
Galatia, 88
Gallio, 88
Garments, 3, 28 f., 34, 56
Gedaliah, seal of, 71, 73
Gerizim, 100
Geshem, 76
Gezer, 28, 48, 53 f., 75
Gezer Calendar, 54 f.
Gibeah, 53, 55, 75
Gilgamesh, 13, 15
Gnostics, 91
Gomorrah, 30
Goshen, 34, 43
Gozan, 60
Granaries, 37
Greek culture, 84
Greek influences, 76, 83
Greek papyri, 88, 91
Gubaru, 75

Habakkuk, 83
Habiru, 29, 41, 101

Hammurabi, 25 ff., 30
Harran, 23, 39, 75, 95
Hazael, 56, 58
Hazor, 28, 46, 54, 59, 99 f.
Hebrew inscriptions, 48, 58 ff., 64
Hebron, 28, 84
Heliopolis, 41
Hermon, Mt., 56
Herod, family of, 80 f.
Herod I (the Great), 81, 84 ff.
Hezekiah, 60 ff., 64
Hieroglyphic script, 38, 48, 97
Hieroglyphs, 38 f., 47 ff.
Hittites, 20, 27 f., 41, 43, 96
Horses, 34, 53 f.
Hoshea, 59, 65
Houses (Ur), 22 f.
Hurrians, 25, 33
Hyksos, 33 f., 41

Incense-altar, 100
Isaiah, 60, 78 ff.
Ishtar gate, 68 f., 72 f.
Ivories, 54 f., 100

Jaazaniah, 58, 73
Jacob, 20, 27, 29, 34, 47
Jarmo, 7
Jehoash, 58
Jehoiachin, 69 f., 72 f., 76
Jehoiakim, 69
Jehu, 6, 56 f.
Jeremiah, 69, 73, 76, 79
Jericho, 7, 29, 46, 84, 97
Jeroboam, 55, 58
Jerusalem, 28, 46, 55, 69 f., 82,
    84, 87, 89, 95 f., 100

Jerusalem, siege of, 60 f., 70
Jeshua, 82
Jesus Christ, 79 ff., 83, 87, 91, 93,
    101
Jewellery, 17, 46 f.
Joahaz, 58
Johanan, 76
Johanna, 82
John, 83, 91
Jonah, 51
Joseph, 33 f., 37, 39, 43, 47, 82
Joshua, 46
Jotham, seal of, 58
Judaean, Hezekiah the, 61
Judas, 82, 87, 89

Kadesh, 43
Karatepe, 96
Karnak, 34, 44, 55, 64
Kawa, 64
Kedar, 69, 76
Khorsabad, 5, 59, 96
King's Highway, 30
Kingu, 8
Kirjath-sephar, 100
Kish, 8, 10 f., 15
Kultepe, 96

Laban, 23, 27
Lachish, 46, 60 ff., 70, 73, 75, 97,
    100
Lamps, 82, 102
Laodicea, 88
Laws, 27
Lazarus, 82
Leather scroll, 48, 66, 78 f.
Lystra, 88

Maccabees, 80
Machpelah, 28, 84
Malta, 88
Mamre, 84
Manasseh, 58, 66
Manuscripts, 91, 93
Marduk, 8, 27, 71
Mari, 23, 25, 30, 97, 100
Martha, 82
Massoretic text, 80
Medes, 69, 75
Megiddo, 13, 28, 53 ff., 58 f., 100
Menahem, 39, 58, 65
Merneptah, 46 f.
Mesha, 55
Mes-kalam-shar, 16 f.
Miriam, 82
Mizpah, 55
Moab, 29, 46, 53 ff.
Moabite stone, 54 f.
Mosaic standard (Ur), 17 ff.
Moses, 44 ff., 48
Murashu, 76

Nabonidus, 20, 75
Nabopolassar, 69
Nash papyrus, 79 f.
Nazareth decree, 81, 83
Nebuchadrezzar, 20, 25, 69 ff., 75
Necho, 69
Negeb, 29, 58, 73, 96
Nero, 82 f., 101
Nimrud, 6, 50 ff., 60, 64 ff., 96 ff.
Nineveh, 7, 13, 50 ff., 60, 62, 64,
    66, 69, 96
Nubia, 41, 44
Nuzi, 25, 27

Oannes, 9

Obelisk, 6, 56 f., 99
Omri, 55 f.
On, 41
Ophel, 53
Ophir, 54
Ossuaries, 82
Oxyrhynchus, 88

Papyrus, 10, 13, 33, 37, 39, 48, 66, 70, 75 f., 79 f., 88, 91, 93
Paradise, 9
Parthenon, 88
Paul, 83 ff., 88, 90 f., 93, 101
Paulus, 88
Pekah, 59, 65
Pen, reed, 48
Pergamum, 88
Persepolis, 76
Petra, 100
Phasaelis, 84
Philip (Herod), 81, 86
Philippi, 88
Philistines, 53
Phoenicia, 55, 58
Pictographic script, 10 f., 24 f.
Pitcher, 99
Pithom, 43
Plagues, 45
Politarchs, 88, 90
Pontius Pilate, 81, 87
Potiphar, 39
Pottery, 46, 82, 98 f., 101
Pottery dating, 97
Pre-flood, 8
Psalms, 79
Ptolemy V, 38

Pul, 58, 65
Pyramid texts, 37

Qarqar, battle of, 56
Qumran, 78 f., 83

Ra'amses, 43
Rameses II, 40 ff.
Ras Shamra, 30, 41, 54, 97, 100
Roll, 37, 91
Rome, 81, 84, 100 f.
Rosetta stone, 38 f., 97
Royal Graves (Ur), 15 ff.

Salome, 82
Samaria, 5, 55, 58 ff., 84, 97
Sammuramat (Semiramis), 56
Sanballat, 76
Sapphira, 82
Saqqarah, 70
Sarah, 27, 29
Sargon of Agade, 12
Sargon II, 5, 59 f.
Scribes, 27, 32 f., 48, 64, 66
Scrolls (Dead Sea), 10, 78 ff., 83, 91
Seal(s), 9, 58, 60, 66, 71, 75
Seal-impression, 73, 75
Sebaste, 84
Semites in Egypt, 28 f., 34 f., 41
Senjirli, 64
Sennacherib, 60 ff.
Shalmaneser III, 6, 56
Shalmaneser V, 59
Sharuhen, 41
Shebanyau, seals of, 58
Shebna (Shebnaiah), 58 ff.

Shechem, 25, 29, 55
Shema', 58
Sherd(s), 46, 54, 58 f., 66, 70
Sheshonq, 55
Shiloh, 53, 100
Shishak (Sheshonq), 55
Shubad, queen, 17
Sidon, 53
Siloam, 61 f., 64
Simon, 82
Sinaitic script, 48
Slaves, 34, 37, 39, 43 f., 51, 58
Sodom, 30
Solomon, 53 f., 84, 100
Statuettes, 99 f.
Stele, 27, 47, 55, 64, 75, 100
Stylus, 10
Sulpicius Quirinius, 80
Sumerians, 7 ff., 19
Synagogue, 89, 100

Taanach, 25, 46
Tabernacle, 100
Tablets, 7, 10 f., 13, 25, 41, 66
Tanis, 43 f.
Taxation, 84
Teacher of Righteousness, 83
Tell el-Amarna, 101
Tell Beit Mirsim, 46, 97
Tell el Far'ah, 55
Tell el Hesi, 97
Tell en-Nasbeh, 55, 58, 73
Tell Qasileh, 53 f.
Tell Tainat, 54
Temple, 54, 76, 84, 92 f., 100
Temple-tower, 17, 20
Teraphim, 100

Thebes, 34, 41, 43, 75
Theodotion, 82
Theodotos, 100
Thessalonica, 88, 90
Tiamat, 8
Tiberius, 80, 87
Tiglath-pileser III, 58, 65 f.
Tirhakah, 61, 64
Tirzah, 55
Titus, 84
Tomb(s), 17, 29 f., 33 f., 37, 42 ff., 60, 76, 81 f., 100 f.
Topographical researches, 96
Treaties, 30, 66 f.
Tuthmosis III, 41
Typology, 101
Tyre, 28, 87, 89

Ubaid, 7, 15
Ugarit (Ras Shamra), 30
Ur, 9, 14 ff., 20, 23, 96
Urartu, 15
Uta-napishtim, 13, 15
Uzziah, 58, 91

Vassal-treaty, 66, 70
Vatican excavations, 100 f.
Vespasian, 87

Wadi Muraba'at, 79
Wadi Qelt, 84
World, map of, 12
Writing, art of, 9 ff., 24 f., 49

Zebulun, 23
Zedekiah, 69 f.
Ziggurat, 17, 20 f., 96
Zoar, 30